Economics and Free Markets

Economics and Free Markets

AN INTRODUCTION

Howard Baetjer Jr.

CATO INSTITUTE
WASHINGTON, D.C.

Chapters 8, 9, 10, and 11 incorporate material previously published in
Free Our Markets: A Citizens' Guide to Essential Economics (2013) with
permission from Jane Philip Publications, LLC.

eBook ISBN: 978-1-944424-51-0
Print ISBN: 978-1-944424-50-3

Library of Congress Cataloging-in-Publication Data available.

Printed in the United States of America.

CATO INSTITUTE
1000 Massachusetts Avenue, N.W.
Washington, D.C. 20001
www.cato.org

CONTENTS

Introduction

That a free economy works at all is one of the most remarkable things in human experience. How can billions of people acting in their individual self-interest—and knowing little about the particular purposes or wishes of others—nevertheless manage to cooperate and produce for one another an ever-increasing abundance of goods and services *with nobody in charge*?

Some basic economic concepts help us understand and appreciate that marvel. The goal of this little book is to present those concepts and thereby help the reader understand why more economic freedom means more human flourishing.

As a primer, the book is intended for people who have not (yet) had the chance to study economics. As a pro-free-market book, it is also for those whose economics courses did not bring out the strong connection between economic freedom and human flourishing.

The book has two main goals. The first is to help the reader learn "the economic way of thinking," the foundational concepts economists use to make sense of the economy. Those concepts, on which the rest of economics is based, are presented in Chapters 1–7: subjective value, scarcity, opportunity cost, thinking "at the margin," comparative advantage, division of labor, and the famous supply and demand.

The second goal is to help readers understand why people need free markets to flourish. The underlying institutions of a *free* market—private ownership and freedom of exchange—are necessary to human well-being for three main reasons, addressed in Chapters 8–11.

First, we need the information that free-market prices give us. Market prices are a kind of telecommunications system; they communicate to everyone what everybody else individually knows about the availability of and need for various goods and services, and thereby they make it possible for us to coordinate our various actions. (We devote all of Chapter 9 to the problems caused by government interference with prices.)

Second, we need free-market profit and loss to guide business enterprise. Profit made in a free market signifies the creation of value for others; loss signifies the destruction of value. In a world where no one can be sure what to do today to make the world a better place tomorrow, this profit-and-loss guidance is indispensable.

Third, we need the incentives that free markets give us to serve others. In free markets, we all must consider the wishes of others in order to get from them what we want, because those others don't have to deal with us. That is not the case where government force may be used to get what we want from others against their wishes. In brief, free markets provide everyone the knowledge, the guidance, and the incentives we need to produce for one another in an extended order of human cooperation.

Economics has great explanatory power. It helps us understand much of what happens in the social world, and how free people benefit others as they seek to benefit themselves. I hope you enjoy this presentation of why that is so.

Part One:

Foundational Concepts

We begin with the concepts that underlie most everything in economics: (a) the nature of value and of wealth, (b) the meaning of scarcity and opportunity cost, (c) the fact that we generally make economic decisions "at the margin," and (d) the benefits we all realize from specializing according to comparative advantage and trading with other specialists for the rest of what we need.

1

Subjective Value and Gains from Trade

We begin this introduction to economics by getting clear on some foundational concepts. In this chapter, we consider the nature of value, the gains we realize from trade, and the unlimited possibilities of wealth creation.

Value Is Subjective

Among the most important concepts in economics is that different people value things differently. Some people love seafood; others dislike it. Some enjoy watching football; others prefer old movies. Tastes in music vary widely. And the same person values the same thing differently in different times and situations. The value you put on a nice meal, for example, depends on how recently you last ate.

The term we use in economics for this fact is that "value is subjective." Value is in the eye of the beholder, so to speak; it is in the person, the subject doing the valuing rather than in the object being valued.

Subjective value stands opposed to the older labor theory of value: the mistaken view (articulated by Adam Smith in *The Wealth of Nations* and taken up by Karl Marx as one of the foundations of his economic theory) that the value of any good is determined by the amount of labor required to produce it. A bottle of water, say, is held to be worth a dollar because a dollar's worth of labor was required to obtain and filter the water, to produce the plastic of the bottle and the lid, to put the water in the bottle, and to produce and glue on its label.

But the labor theory of value is untenable. If it were true, then an apple pie that took four hours to produce would be worth the same amount as a mud pie that took the same four hours. It's not, because people don't like to eat mud. The tastes and preferences of the people doing the valuing are what determine something's value.

Voluntary Trade Creates Wealth, Makes Traders Wealthier According to Their Own Values

That value is subjective has a wonderful consequence: people can make one another better off merely through trading, through exchange. When Jimmy prefers Ted's backpack to his own skateboard, and Ted prefers Jimmy's skateboard to his own backpack, the boys can exchange backpack for skateboard and make each boy better off according to his own subjective values. In an important sense, each boy is wealthier after the trade. When crabbers in my home state of Maryland trade blue crabs to Washington State apple growers for their apples, both groups are better off—wealthier according to their different values—as each group gives up what it values less for what it values more.

Notice how this insight about the mutual benefits from voluntary exchange contradicts the widespread notion that exchange is zero-sum, that in a market economy, some people benefit at the expense of others. The notion is there in the expression "the rich get richer and the poor get poorer." That implies that the rich get rich at the expense of the poor. We hear "one man's loss is another man's gain," as if there is only a certain amount to go around, so that if one person becomes better off, someone else must have become worse off. Underlying a lot of the animus against "haves" is the notion— perhaps unconscious and unexamined—that the wealth of "haves" comes at the expense of "have-nots."

But that is not true, as long as the wealthy earn their wealth in voluntary exchange (rather than through special privileges from government, such as bailouts, subsidies, or protected monopolies). Consider Steve Jobs, LeBron James, and Beyoncé. They are all "haves." Did they become wealthy at the expense of the rest of us? Not at all. They became wealthy by delighting us with their electronic devices, athletic prowess, and great songs and videos.

Invisible Hand Principle

That participants in voluntary exchange mutually benefit one another is so important that it can hardly be overemphasized. It has this important corollary: in a free and competitive economy, people who want more for themselves are guided, as if by an invisible hand, to benefit others. Why? Because in a free society, others don't have to interact with us at all. If we want something from others, we must persuade them to give it to us by offering them something they value more in return. In the words of my grad school professor Walter Williams: "In a free market, you get more for yourself by serving your fellow man. You don't have to care about him! Just serve him."

We call this the "invisible hand principle" after Adam Smith's statement in *The Wealth of Nations* that although a person engaged in commerce may "intend . . . only his own gain, . . . he is in this, as in many other cases, led by an invisible hand to promote an end which was no part of his intention," namely, to promote the public interest.

Wealth Is Not Fixed; People Create It and Can Do So without Limit

Virtually all wealth is created by human ingenuity and effort. A few good things come to us for free—the blessed rain, the sunshine, and the air we breathe come to mind—all the rest we must create. Houses, farms, backhoes, clothing, soap, oil refineries, flat-screen TVs, and every other good thing that supports and enriches our lives we humans create by transforming raw materials. The physical stuff from which we fashion those things has always been here, but through the application of our ingenuity, we transform that physical stuff into goods and services we value.

This process has no apparent limit because the ability to create new wealth is bounded only by the human imagination, and humans are endlessly imaginative.

The Ultimate Resource

Some people worry that human wealth and well-being are limited by the finiteness of physical resources, such as oil, metals, and arable land. The worry is needless because, as economist Julian Simon has taught us, the ultimate resource is the human imagination coupled with the human spirit. Human imagination ceaselessly finds new and better ways to satisfy human wants and needs. It literally creates resources; it finds ways to do more with less; it finds substitutes for resources as they get more expensive.

In what sense do people literally create resources? They do so by discovering how physical stuff once considered useless can in fact be used. Consider the sticky black stuff that used to gunk up streams in Pennsylvania and Oklahoma: petroleum. That was not a resource until creatively thinking human beings discovered that it could be refined into kerosene, gasoline, and the like. That discovery turned petroleum into a resource.

Consider the vast lakes of shale, miles below the earth's surface, until recently considered useless. Those lakes were turned into a valuable resource when people discovered that with horizontal drilling and hydraulic fracturing ("fracking"), we can profitably extract great quantities of oil and natural gas from them.

The ultimate resource—the human imagination coupled with the human spirit—is constantly finding us ways to do more with less. I remember when it took a strong man to crush a beer can in his hand, because beer cans were made of thick metal. But people discovered how to make cans with metal so much thinner and lighter—and therefore less expensive—that now anyone can crush a beer can. I remember concerns that LP record albums, the leading technology for recording music, would become terribly expensive as the cost of the vinyl used to make them was rising. Those albums also took up a lot of space in my cabinet. Then came compact discs, which held many more songs in less space than a vinyl record. And now I can store *hundreds* of songs on an SD card little larger than a fingertip.

I used to lug heavy books with me to read on vacation. Now I can take all the books I want on my Kindle, the size of one thin paperback. People endlessly discover ways to do more with less.

And we develop substitutes, often better and cheaper than what we used before. Consider transoceanic telephone calls. They used to be carried by copper cable, tons of copper torn out of the mountains of Idaho and Peru and laid across the ocean at great expense. The calls themselves were expensive and of poor quality, with delays and signal loss. But the human imagination found substitutes for copper cable—optical fiber and satellites—that carry hundreds of times more phone calls inexpensively, at the speed of light, and with virtually no signal loss. And the optical fibers, like SD cards, are made of cheap and abundant sand.

And as former Saudi Arabian oil minister Sheikh Zaki Yamani said three decades ago, "The Stone Age did not end for lack of stone, and the Oil Age will end long before the world runs out of oil." Human imagination coupled with the human spirit will find a replacement for oil. I wonder what it will be.

Money Is Not Wealth

Let us finish this chapter with the important distinction between money and wealth. Of course, in a money economy, having more money makes one wealthier, other things remaining equal. Nevertheless, strictly speaking, money is not wealth. We can't eat it, wear it, build shelters with it, or listen to MP3s with it. Money's great value to us is as a medium of exchange. It frees us from the limitations of barter. We don't value money in itself, but for what it can buy. As economist Antony Davies says, "Money is just the conveyor belt." Ultimately, we trade goods and services not for money, but for other goods and services.

In this book, when we think about wealth, let's think about the goods and services we value—what Adam Smith called the "necessaries and conveniences of life"—and not about money.

2

Scarcity and Opportunity Cost

Scarcity

Another of the foundational concepts of economics is scarcity. In Thomas Sowell's words:[1] "What does 'scarce' mean? It means that people want more than there is." In the words of my textbook, scarcity means "there is less of a good freely available from nature than people would like." Sowell again: "There has never been enough to satisfy everyone completely. That is what scarcity means."

Scarcity is not rareness: Cars are not rare; they are everywhere. But they are scarce nonetheless because not everyone who wants one has one, and not everyone who wants two has two.

Virtually all goods are scarce. In fact, the only good I can think of that is not scarce is air. We breathe in all we want, freely available from nature. We might think that water is not scarce, but even outside drought-stricken areas, clean, drinkable water surely is.

To appreciate scarcity and its significance, focus on the scarcity of productive resources: the land, human talent, and capital goods—buildings, machinery, and equipment—we require for producing what people want. We have unlimited desires for goods and services, but the land, labor, and capital available to produce them are all limited at any particular time. They are scarce. Accordingly, so are the goods and services we can produce with them.

This insight is at the heart of economics. Because there are not enough resources with which to produce everything we want at any time, we must decide how to allocate those resources and thereby decide to produce some goods instead of others. We constantly face such tradeoffs, because if we use resources to produce one thing, we can't use them to produce another instead. How we make those choices (and, implicitly, who makes them) is what economics is about. As Sowell says, "Economics is the study of the use of scarce resources which have alternative uses."

That is a helpful definition, one to keep in mind throughout this book.

Rationing

The next principle follows from the fact of scarcity: scarcity necessitates rationing. Rationing is the allocation of scarce resources among their myriad possible uses. We can't avoid rationing, but we can choose how to do it.

Think of all the ways in which we humans can ration goods. Sadly, we often do it by force—the biggest and strongest just take what they want. We sometimes do it by equal division, in which everyone gets the same share. We can do it by some kind of lottery in which chance determines who gets what. Some things we ration on a first come, first served basis. Sometimes some of us give goods or services to the smartest (e.g., scholarships) or the neediest (e.g., charity).

In a free society in which property rights are respected, it's up to the owner of a good or service to decide how it will be rationed, and often private owners do give some of their property away to the deserving or needy. In a free-market economy, however, most of the time goods and services are rationed according to buyers' *willingness and ability to pay the market price*. Goods and resources go to those who will pay that price.

The great advantage of this means of rationing is that it tends to get goods and services to the people who value them most, who can put them to the highest valued uses. The tendency is not perfect because sometimes those who value goods most don't have (and can't borrow) enough money to pay the market price. That's a real drawback of rationing by price.

But that drawback is offset many times over by the way price rationing tends to get goods to where they will do the most good for real human beings.

Opportunity Cost

A crucial concept bound up with all we have been saying about scarcity is opportunity cost.

Let's start with some examples: If you were not reading this passage right now, what's the next best thing you could be doing instead? Whatever that is, its value (to you) is your opportunity cost of reading this passage. I ask my students what they would have chosen to do had they not come to class that day. Usually the answer is "sleeping"; next most frequent is "working." (Only in third place, sadly, is "studying.") In each case, the value to the particular student of the sleeping, the working, or the studying she gives up is her opportunity cost of coming to class.

An easy-to-remember definition of opportunity cost is "whatever you give up." A more precise definition focuses not on the thing given up, but on its *value*. Opportunity cost, then, is *the value of the best alternative forgone* when one takes an action. In a world of scarcity, every choice any of us ever makes has a cost, because when we choose to do A, we cannot do B instead. The cost to a farmer of growing wheat might be the value to him of growing soybeans instead. The cost to Ben and Jerry's of producing a batch of Cherry Garcia ice cream might be the value of producing a batch of Chunky Monkey instead. The cost to a student of going to college might be the forgone income and experience from working at a job instead, plus the value to him of all the things he could have purchased with what he spends on tuition.

Strictly speaking, actions have costs, but things do not. When you buy a bottle of water for $1.25, strictly speaking it is not the bottle that has a cost but your purchase of it: what's the next best thing you could have done with the $1.25 (and the time it takes you to make the purchase)? The value to you of that next best thing is the cost (to you) of purchasing the water.

Notice also that the same action has different costs to different people and to the same person at different times. The reason is that opportunity costs are *values* (of the next best opportunities forgone), and values, as we have seen, are *subjective*. For example, the cost of studying economics on a Sunday afternoon in the fall will be much higher to a pro football lover who is offered a free ticket to his favorite team's game than it will be to someone who has little else to do that afternoon.

Costs vary according to situation. The cost of growing a hundred bushels of wheat will be lower to a farmer with excellent soil and adequate rain than it will be to a farmer with poor soil in a dry region. The latter farmer can still produce that much wheat, but he'll have to use additional scarce resources of fertilizer, water, and irrigation equipment to do so. The value of the next best uses of that fertilizer, water, and irrigation equipment—perhaps on other farms and crops—is the additional opportunity cost of growing wheat on poor, dry soil.

Every action has a cost. Nothing is free. "Free public education," for example, is not free. It uses up buildings, desks, electricity, teachers' time and expertise, and other resources. The value of all the other goods and services that could be produced with those resources is the opportunity cost of public education.

3

Thinking at the Margin

Many of the choices we make concern doing more or less of something. Should we have another slice of pie, or not? Should we hit the snooze button on our alarm clocks or get up now? Most of my students sign up for at least four courses each term and then choose whether or not to take one more.

The term we use in economics for the additional piece of pie, the extra few minutes of sleep, or the fifth course is "marginal." Marginal means additional, one more or one less.

Economic thinking is marginal thinking. We generally make decisions "at the margin" (whether or not we are aware of doing so) by comparing the benefits and opportunity costs of doing a little more or a little less of something. Economics focuses on those "marginal benefits" and "marginal costs." The marginal benefit of the extra pie is the pleasure of eating it; the marginal cost is (the value of) staying slimmer and not feeling stuffed. The marginal benefit of the extra sleep is that sweet added rest; the marginal cost is (the value of) getting going on the day promptly. The marginal benefit of taking a fifth course is more learning and additional credits toward a student's degree; its marginal cost is (the value of) the studying for other courses, the working, sleeping, or socializing the student could do otherwise.

Thinking in relation to the margin has been important in economics. It was the key to solving the "water–diamonds paradox" that had puzzled people for years: why is water, necessary for life itself, so inexpensive, whereas diamonds, used mostly for decoration, are so expensive? The key is that we value "at the margin"; that is, we value not the entirety of a good that may exist in the world at some time, but rather a little more or a little less of it. It is surely true that people value water *on the whole* much more than they value diamonds *on the whole*. But given that water is plentiful, how much is a person willing to pay for an additional (marginal) gallon? Not very much. Given that diamonds are rare, how much is a person willing to pay for additional (marginal) diamond? A great deal. The total value of all water to mankind is almost infinitely high, whereas the total value of all diamonds is much lower. But "at the margins" on which we find ourselves, with abundant water and few diamonds, the marginal value of diamonds exceeds the marginal value of water.

Good economic thinking distinguishes marginal costs and benefits from total or average costs and benefits. Let's take a couple of examples to illustrate.

Imagine a student the day before her final exam in microeconomics; she wants to study hard for it. But suppose she has recently fallen into a spring romance with a young man who has just finished all his exams. He proposes that they spend the evening together, walking and smooching amidst the blossoms in the balmy spring air. Suppose she tells him that she would love to, but she has to study for her micro final, and he replies, "What's more important, our relationship or economics?"

Can you see what's invalid (and perhaps manipulative) in his question? It asks her to choose between their relationship and her economics course. But what's at stake is not the *total value* of the relationship or the economics course, but a *marginal* three hours spent on one or the other. If the young woman has her wits about her, and if she has learned to think at the margin, she might answer this way: "My dear, if I had to choose between our relationship and economics, I would definitely choose our relationship, even if it meant failing! But just for this one evening, it's more important that I study."

Here's a tricky question to clarify the difference between "marginal" and "average":

Suppose the total cost to Southwest Airlines of a flight from Baltimore to Providence, Rhode Island, is about $5,000, a little more or less depending on fuel consumption and the numbers of sodas and snacks consumed. Suppose the aircraft carries 100 passengers, but this particular flight is not full. Suppose you come running up to the ticket counter shortly before departure time and ask to get aboard. What's the minimum price at which Southwest Airlines can benefit from selling you a ticket?

You might reason this way: If the total cost of the flight is $5,000 and the plane holds 100 passengers, then the average cost per passenger on a full flight would be $50. At any price below $50, Southwest could not cover its average cost; it would necessarily lose money on the flight. Therefore, the airline should charge at least $50.

That would not be good economic thinking because it focuses on the average cost rather than on the marginal cost. Keep in mind that the plane is going to make the trip. The other passengers have paid for their tickets. The total they have paid may be more or less than the $5,000 necessary to cover the total cost. That does not matter at this point either, any more than the average cost matters. How much would the airline need to charge you, now, at the last minute, in order to benefit? To answer, think at the margin.

What is the marginal cost to Southwest of taking you to Providence? That is, what additional scarce resources must the airline use to get you there? Your additional mass will require the plane to burn additional fuel to move it; of course, your additional mass is just a ten-thousandth or so of the total mass, so just a ten-thousandth more fuel should be needed. Call it $1's worth of fuel. Then there's the soda you would drink and the little bags of pretzels and peanuts you would eat. Southwest buys them in bulk, and not much in the way of resources is needed to produce them. Call it another $1. That's it. The marginal cost to Southwest of taking you to Providence, then, would be $2. If the airline charges you even $3, its marginal benefit of $3 would exceed its marginal cost of $2.

I don't mean to say that it would be wise, all things considered, for airlines to price last-minute seats on this kind of reasoning. They may have weighty reasons for sticking to posted prices, in order to head off strategic behavior by clever passengers trying to get a seat for much less than they would be willing to pay. But it's a good example for illustrating the difference between marginal costs and benefits and average costs and benefits. On that one flight, at least, Southwest could benefit by $1 by selling you a $3 ticket.

Let's push the thought experiment a step further, however. Suppose Southwest *did* have a policy of selling empty seats at the last minute for any price that exceeded its (estimated) marginal cost of, say, $2. What would the price likely turn out to be, in practice? Probably not $2. Suppose the opportunity to get a great deal attracted not just you but also me, each of us hoping to get, let us suppose, the one remaining seat on the flight. You offer $3. I offer $4. You counter with $5, and I jump impatiently to $10. Where would the bidding stop? Well, suppose that getting to Providence on that particular flight is worth $70 to you but $90 to me. You would only bid up to $70, and I'd get the ticket for something between $70 and $90, depending on how cleverly I judged your willingness to pay (and the patience of the gate agent). Like Southwest Airlines, each of us would be thinking and acting at the margin, bidding one more dollar as long as the benefit to us of doing so—getting on that flight—is greater than the cost—paying the whole bid.

The Rule of Rational Life

A handy way to remember what it means to think at the margin is what my former colleague Jerry German called the "Rule of Rational Life": as long as marginal benefit is greater than marginal cost, do it. That applies to the second piece of pie, the extra sleep, the additional course, the time studying for a microeconomics final, letting people get on a flight to Providence, and bidding to get on that flight. You'll find that it applies to every decision you ever make, as long as you think clearly about the relevant margins and all the costs and benefits involved.

Nuances of "Marginal"

Before finishing with a rather painful illustration of why marginal costs and benefits matter more to decisionmaking than average or total costs and benefits, let's consider an important nuance to the meaning of "marginal."

In much of the thinking we do about the economy, it is helpful to think about the marginal units of something or other as being identical to all the other units. We imagine, for example, that the second piece of pie we might have for dessert is identical to the first, that an additional 10 minutes of sleep is just as restful as the 10 minutes before our alarm went off, that the fifth course we might take in a term is just as valuable as the fourth, and so on. Thought about that way, "marginal" means strictly "additional," and each additional unit is identical to the one before.

But "marginal" has another sense in which additional units are actually not as good. The marginal 10 minutes of sleep we get after hitting our alarm clock's snooze button are generally not as satisfying as those before because of guilt over not getting up and dread of the next alarm. Similarly, marginal hours of studying late at night are often not as valuable as we tire and lose concentration. Students enroll in the courses they value most first, so a marginal fifth course is unlikely to be as valuable in the student's subjective judgment as the first four. When a farmer decides to put additional acres into cultivation in a season, those marginal acres will be on the parts of his farm with less fertile soil, some drainage problems, or other drawbacks.

Hence the word "marginal" also has the sense of being not quite up to par, not as desirable.

Example: The Welfare Trap

Because most of our decisions are made on margins of one kind or another, we respond to incentives at the margin rather than on the whole or on average. A painful illustration of this fact is what is called "the welfare trap," the way in which marginal changes in earned income affect changes in disposable income for families on welfare. As a poor mother of two, say, earns more through working at a job, she gradually loses eligibility for welfare benefits, such as TANF (Temporary Assistance for Needy Families, a cash benefit), food stamps, housing assistance, and the like. Economists use the (slightly misleading) term "marginal tax rate" to refer to the proportion of additional earnings a person loses, either through increased taxes or lost welfare benefits. (It's misleading because lost benefits are not taxes paid. Nevertheless, that is the term used.)

The devilish problem is that the *marginal* tax rates that low-income earners face—through the phasing out of benefits and increased taxes—can give them a strong disincentive to earn more, even though the *average* tax rate they pay does not seem to be much of a disincentive to work.

The following illustration comes from "Modeling Potential Income and Welfare Assistance Benefits in Illinois," a report published by the Illinois Policy Institute in 2014.

Let's start the example with this question: Would a poor mother of two have an incentive to take a job offering $15 an hour—or $31,200 a year before taxes—if she could also bring home an additional $29,500 in government assistance after taxes for a total annual income of $60,700?

I assume that most would say yes, that's a good deal. But we are thinking about totals when we ask the question that way, not about marginal changes. Such a person would almost never face a choice between not working at all and working at $15 an hour. She would more likely face a choice about whether or not to take another step up the job ladder, going to that $15 an hour from, say, $12 an hour as she gets more training and takes on additional responsibility. *At the margin*, how strong is her incentive to do that?

Table 3.1 shows how a low-income, working Chicagoan's take-home income would change with incremental changes

Table 3.1.
The Welfare Trap for a Family of Three in Chicago, 2014

Hourly wage	Gross earned income	Refundable tax credits	Cash assistance	Food assistance	Housing assistance	Childcare assistance	Medical assistance	ACA premium tax credit	Taxes	Net earned income + benefits
$0	$0		Yes	Yes	Yes		Yes		Yes	$36,424
$8.25	$17,160	Yes	→	→	→	Yes	–		→	$63,191
$10.00	$20,800	→	0	→	→	→	–		→	$63,283
$12.00	$24,960	→		→	→	→	–		→	$63,597
$15.00	$31,200	→		→	→	→	→	Yes	→	$60,701
$18.00	$37,440	→		0	0	0	–	→	→	$39,332
$21.00	$43,680	→					→	0	→	$41,075
...	...									
$38.00	$79,040								→	$63,200

Note: ACA = Affordable Care Act.

30

in his or her earned income, starting from the current Chicago minimum wage rate of $8.25. Note that if a mother such as we are considering were currently earning $12 an hour and receiving the government benefits to which she is entitled, taking the raise to $15 an hour and thereby increasing her earned income by $6,240 a year would mean decreasing her take-home income by $2,896 a year! Her gain in earned income would be more than offset by her loss of government assistance. That's a marginal tax rate of over 100 percent. Thinking at the margin, does she have an incentive to take that $3-an-hour raise or to refuse it?

Although it is dreadful to contemplate, note that the problem is worst, in the Chicago case, for a raise from $15 an hour to $18 an hour, where the marginal tax rate is over 340 percent. And note that not until she was earning $38 an hour would such a mother take home more than she was taking home when she was earning minimum wage.

Just think what those marginal tax rates do to the incentives of poor people to work their way out of poverty. It is not surprising that so many people get trapped in welfare. In fact, to me it's impressive—it makes me proud of the human race—that despite those awful incentives at the margin, so many people do climb up the job ladder, bear the losses of disposable income, and raise themselves out of poverty.

4

Division of Labor and Comparative Advantage

Specialization, Division of Labor, and Trade

Human beings are the only species that trades. We have already seen that because value is subjective and different people value things differently, we can create value (or wealth) for one another simply by mutually trading what we value less for what we value more. One of the remarkable things about human society is that we don't produce primarily for ourselves and take advantage of chance opportunities to trade. Rather, we produce almost exclusively for others, expecting to get almost everything we want for ourselves through trade with others who have produced for us.

The world economy is a fantastic network of human cooperation in which all of us specialize in producing just one or a few things abundantly, confident that others will do the same in their different and complementary specialties. Through this worldwide specialization and division of labor—assuming we have a well-functioning price system to keep it all coordinated—we can produce for one another a gloriously high and rising standard of living.

Science writer Matt Ridley provides a glimpse of the system in *The Rational Optimist*:

> As I write this, it is nine o'clock in the morning. In the two hours since I got out of bed I have showered in water heated by North Sea gas, shaved using an American razor running on electricity made from British coal, eaten a slice of bread made from French wheat, spread with New Zealand butter and Spanish marmalade, then brewed a cup of tea using leaves grown in Sri Lanka, dressed myself in clothes of Indian cotton and Australian wool, with shoes of Chinese leather and Malaysian rubber, and read a newspaper made from Finnish wood pulp and Chinese ink.

Specialization, division of labor, and trade: as much as anything else, these explain our success as a species and our steadily rising standard of living. Let's look more closely at why.

Why Specialization and Trade Increase Output

One way specialization and trade help people prosper is by letting everyone take advantage of productive resources present in one area but not in others. Which region should specialize in producing blue crabs, for example, Maryland or Iowa? Maryland, obviously, because Maryland has the Chesapeake Bay. It would be possible to produce crabs in Iowa, perhaps in huge aquariums with seawater trucked in from the coasts, but that would make no sense because it would be so expensive. Better to take advantage of the Chesapeake, letting nature provide the environment where crabs thrive. Iowa should specialize in producing wheat, because it has wonderfully broad, fertile fields in which to grow it. Marylanders and Iowans should and do trade crabs for wheat.

Similarly, Florida should produce oranges; Brazil, coffee; and Switzerland, skiing, to take advantage of each nation's special natural resources.

But taking advantage of particular natural resources is not the most important reason for specializing and trading. Specializing by itself increases our productivity—our output per person—because when people specialize, they develop deeper skills and better tools and take advantage of scale economies.

Deeper skills. This consequence of specialization hardly needs comment. When we specialize in some task or job (or sport), we get lots of practice doing it, and with practice comes skill. Think of skilled welders, carpenters, pianists, nurses, truck drivers, and pilots; their skill comes from each worker's specializing in his or her particular job.

Better tools. Specialists at any task or job tend to notice and invent ways of doing that job that save them effort. They figure out improvements to tools and processes and sometimes entirely new ones. Those innovative technologies improve their productivity. Farmers and artificial turf installers use lasers to help them level their fields. Retailers use barcodes to manage inventory. Shippers invented the container and container ship to speed loading and unloading. Fishers use liquid nitrogen to "flash freeze" their catch to keep it fresh. Specialists innovate.

Economies of scale. Specialization, with help of innovative technologies, allows for astonishing economies of scale. The point of dividing up the labor of a production process—with different people specializing in its different aspects using the best available tools—is to produce on a larger scale and thereby at a lower unit cost. Adam Smith gave the classic example in his account of the pin factory:

> One man draws out the wire; another straights it; a third cuts it; a fourth points it; a fifth grinds it at the top for receiving the head; to make the head requires two or three distinct operations; to put it on is a peculiar business; to whiten the pins is another; it is even a trade by itself to put them into the paper; and the important business of making a pin is, in this manner, divided into about eighteen distinct operations, which, in some manufactories, are all performed by distinct hands.

This specialization and the development of special tools suited to each task in the process allow for greatly increased productivity:

> I have seen a small manufactory of this kind, where ten men only were employed, and where some of them consequently performed two or three distinct operations. But though they were very poor, and therefore but indifferently accommodated with the necessary machinery, they could, when they exerted themselves, make among them about twelve pounds

of pins in a day. There are in a pound upwards of four thousand pins of a middling size. Those ten persons, therefore, could make among them upwards of forty-eight thousand pins in a day. Each person, therefore, making a tenth part of forty-eight thousand pins, might be considered as making four thousand eight hundred pins in a day. But if they had all wrought separately and independently, and without any of them having been educated to this peculiar business, they certainly could not each of them have made twenty, perhaps not one pin in a day.

In our day, scale economies are even more obvious. Frito-Lay specializes in snack foods, Ford in vehicles, Boeing in jet airliners. When you get a chance, take a tour of a modern potato chip or SUV or airliner factory and marvel at the highly trained workers and magnificent machinery that simultaneously increase quantity, improve quality, and reduce cost, relative to what could be accomplished on a smaller scale.

Comparative Advantage

It is easy to see the benefits of trade between regions with different skills and natural resources. Maryland should produce crabs and exchange them for wheat produced in Iowa. Each state is "better" at producing its particular product in that it can produce it at a lower resource cost than the other state—it needs to devote fewer scarce resources to producing that product. Being better in this sense we call "absolute advantage." Similarly, Brazil has an absolute advantage over most places in producing coffee, Switzerland in producing skiing, and Florida in producing oranges. Obviously, a goodly portion of the people in those regions should specialize in those products and trade them to people in other places with different absolute advantages.

But what about places that are so resource poor that they have an absolute advantage in nothing; can they still benefit from specializing and trading? If so, in what should they specialize? And what about places that are so resource rich that they have absolute advantages over other regions in everything? Should they produce everything for themselves? Or can they also benefit from specializing and trading?

Those questions were answered in the early 19th century by English economist David Ricardo, in what has come to be called the "law of comparative advantage." Ricardo showed that *all* people and regions can benefit one another through specialization and trade. The key is to specialize in producing those goods for which one has a *comparative advantage*, as distinct from absolute advantage. All people and regions have a comparative advantage in something (or some things); they should specialize in that (or those).

The benefits of specializing according to comparative advantage and trading can be illustrated with a simple arithmetic example that imagines just two countries, Japan and the United States, and two goods, food and clothing. We assume for simplicity that worker time is the only resource needed to produce them.[2]

Let us suppose that the workers of the two countries can produce food and clothing at the rates presented in Table 4.1.

Table 4.1. Output per Worker Day, Japan and United States

	Output per worker day (units)	
	Food	Clothing
Japan (50 million workers)	3	9
United States (200 million workers)	2	1

Let's consider two scenarios, the first without trade and with half of each country's workforce producing food and the other half producing clothing. In that case, as Table 4.2 shows, the Japanese would produce 75 million units of food and 225 million units of clothing each day. Because they don't trade, that's also what they could consume. The United States would produce and consume 200 million units of food and 100 million units of clothing each day. Total output would be 275 million units of food and 325 units of clothing per day.

Table 4.2. Total Production and Consumption without Trade, Japan and United States

	Total production and consumption without trade, with half the workforce producing each good	
	Food	Clothing
Japan (50 million workers)	25 million × 3 = 75 million	25 million × 9 = 225 million
United States (200 million workers)	100 million × 2 = 200 million	100 million × 1 = 100 million
Total output	275 million	325 million

Now look at what happens if all the Japanese produce the good in the production of which they have the larger absolute advantage (Table 4.3). That's clothing, because the Japanese are nine times more productive than Americans in producing clothing but just half again more productive in producing food. And suppose at the same time, the Americans concentrate on producing the good in which they have the smaller absolute *dis*advantage. That's food, because although Americans are worse at producing both goods, they are much closer to the Japanese in producing food than in producing clothing. Japan would then produce 450 million units of clothing, while

ECONOMICS AND FREE MARKETS: AN INTRODUCTION

the United States would produce 400 units of food each day. Look at how much larger total output is!

Table 4.3. Total Production with Comparative Advantage, Japan and United States

| | Total production with each country producing the good in which it has a comparative advantage | |
	Food	Clothing
Japan (50 million workers)	0	50 million × 9 = 450 million
United States (200 million workers)	200 million × 2 = 400 million	0
Total output	400 million	450 million

Now, suppose that each country splits its *output* in half, keeping half for itself and trading the rest to the other country for half of *its* output (Table 4.4). Look at what happens to consumption.

Table 4.4. Total Consumption with Comparative Advantage and Trade, Japan and United States

| | Total consumption with specialization according to comparative advantage and trade | |
	Food	Clothing
Japan (50 million workers)	200 million	225 million
United States (200 million workers)	200 million	225 million
Total output	400 million	450 million

Japan could now consume 200 million units of food instead of only 75 million, while consuming the same amount of clothing it did before. The United States could consume the same 200 million units of food, but 225 units of clothing instead of only 100 million.

The example illustrates the magic of trade. When countries, regions, or individuals specialize according to their comparative advantage, everyone can have more. This point is of the utmost importance: when people specialize according to comparative advantage and trade with one another, *there is more to go around. People live better.* It's worth mentioning that on this point, there is virtually no disagreement among economists.

How do we determine a trading partner's comparative advantage? I recommend any of three ways.

First (my favorite, intentionally ungrammatical so as to be memorable), do what you are more better at or less worse at. In our example, the Japanese are absolutely better at producing both food and clothing, but they are "more better" at producing clothing, so their comparative advantage lies in clothing. Americans are worse at both, but "less worse" in producing food, so their comparative advantage lies in food.

Second, compare absolute advantages or absolute disadvantages; one's comparative advantage is that in which one has the larger absolute advantage or smaller absolute disadvantage.

Third (the formal, textbook-approved way), find the good the country (or region or person) can produce at the lower opportunity cost (as opposed to resource cost); that is where its comparative advantage lies. For example, it costs Japan nine units of clothing to produce one unit of food, because the worker producing the food is *not* producing the nine units of clothing she could produce in the same time instead. But it costs the United States just half a unit of clothing to produce a unit of food, because the American worker producing the food could produce only half a unit of clothing in that time instead. Because the United States has the lower opportunity cost of producing each unit of food (just half a unit of clothing forgone to Japan's nine units of clothing forgone), it has the comparative advantage in food.

Don't get lost in the arithmetic. Do remember the lesson: everyone can be made better off when we specialize according to comparative advantage and trade with one another. The more freely people trade, the better we live.

Part Two:

Demand and Supply

The best tool in the economist's toolkit is supply-and-demand analysis. Thinking in relation to supply and demand helps us understand how market prices are determined and how they change to reflect changing conditions.

In these next chapters, we'll consider first demand, then supply, then how their interaction determines market price and quantity at any particular time. We'll finish with some practice, representing how changes in supply and demand cause changes in prices and quantities sold.

5

Demand

Demand and Demand Curves

The basic principle of demand is totally familiar to every reader, even those who have not studied economics. To illustrate, imagine a clothing store with a lot of winter coats on the racks as spring approaches. What will the store probably do to get rid of those coats? It will put them on sale, of course. The lower price will give customers a stronger incentive to buy the coats, so the store will sell more of them. Everyone who understands that scenario understands the "law of demand," which holds that, other factors remaining equal, *a greater quantity of a good will be sold at lower prices than at higher prices.*

We use "demand" to refer to the actual and potential buyers in a particular market and the prices they are willing to pay. Let's create a simple example of a market for bottled water.

Because value is subjective (see Chapter 1), different buyers are willing to pay different amounts of money for a good at any time. Notice, too, that each of us is willing to pay less for each additional ("marginal") unit of a good than we'd pay for the one before. A first bottle of water, for example, might be quite important to us for slaking our thirst, but having slaked that thirst, we would value a second bottle less highly, and a third less highly still. (This fact that each additional unit of a good has less value to a person than the one before is the principle of "diminishing marginal utility.")

In any market we have numerous different buyers, each with different values for additional units of the good, all spread out across the region. How can we organize in our minds all those different buyers, with all their different preferences, so as to think about them helpfully? In economics, we arrange them in our imaginations—and onto the demand "curves" we draw—according to their willingness to pay. In effect, we line them up from most willing to pay, to next most willing to pay, to next most willing to pay, and so on.

We represent that arrangement on a simple graph that plots willingness to pay—the value to buyers—along with quantity.

To make up a simple example, suppose we have five people watching a Little League Baseball game on a warm day, so they would like to have some water. Table 5.1 shows the maximum each person would be willing to pay for a first bottle of water, then a second, and then a third.

Table 5.1. Willingness to Pay

Name	Value—maximum price each is willing to pay
Arthur	$2 for a first bottle, $1 for a second, $0 for a third
Betsy	$7 for a first bottle, $3 for a second, $1 for a third
Charlie	$10 for a first bottle, $6 for a second, $0 for a third
Donna	$4 for a first bottle, $3 for a second, $0.50 for a third
Ellie	$9 for a first bottle, $4 for a second, $2 for a third

Expressed in table form, the information is difficult to interpret, so we organize it by lining up the buyers in a graph according to their willingness to pay (Figure 5.1).

By convention, in supply-and-demand graphs, we put everything that can be represented in money—particularly value, cost, and price—on the vertical axis; and we put quantities of the good or service on the horizontal axis. Here, our value dimension is the value to the different buyers of additional bottles of water. We can also think of value to buyers as their willingness to pay, or the highest price each person would be willing to pay if he or she

Figure 5.1
Demand Example: Bottles of Water

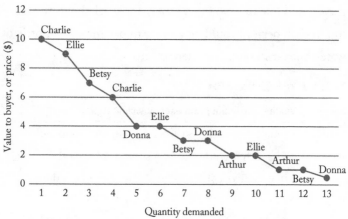

had to go that high. Our quantity dimension is numbers of bottles of water. (Note that quantities represented on the horizontal axes of supply-and-demand graphs are almost always, implicitly, quantities per period of time, in this case, during the baseball game.)

This arrangement—the jagged line in Figure 5.1—we call a demand "curve." (Yes, we call it a curve even when it is jagged or straight.) Note that its downward slope reflects the law of demand: at higher prices, fewer bottles would be wanted; at lower prices, more bottles would be wanted.

Almost never will a demand curve identify the demander of each unit by name, as in our example here. Almost always, we think about markets with so many potential buyers that we can't begin to name them all, so the curve will be just a downward-sloping line. I introduce demand with the names and values of the demanders, however, to emphasize that every point on every demand curve always represents some particular person willing to pay some particular amount (and no more) for one more unit of the good or service. Keep this in mind. Economics is not about lines and points and areas on graphs. It's about people and the exchanges they make. When you look at a demand curve, "see" the people on it.

The Information a Demand Curve Provides

A demand curve gives us two useful kinds of information: (a) quantity information about values and (b) value information about quantities. For example, what does it tell us about a buyer value of $6? To answer, we look across from the $6 level on the value axis to the demand curve, where we see that $6 corresponds to a quantity of four. That tells us that only four bottles of water in this imaginary market are valued at $6 or more. If the price were $5, how many bottles would people be willing to buy? Still only four, because Donna and Ellie would not be willing to buy the fifth and sixth unless the price got down to \$4. At a price of \$4, six bottles would be purchased because six bottles have a value of \$4 or more.

To generalize from these examples: *a demand curve tells us the quantity demanded at any price*, the quantity that people in the market would be willing and able to buy at that price.

Now let's start with quantity rather than price. What does a demand curve tell us about any additional water bottle that might be sold? For example, what does it tell us about the seventh bottle that might be sold, after the first six had been bought by those who valued them most? Well, trace a line upward from seven on the quantity axis and see where your eye crosses the demand curve. It crosses at a value to the buyer of \$3. That means that the seventh bottle has a value of \$3 to Betsy or Donna, the next (the marginal) buyer. What's the value of the 13th bottle that might be sold in this market? Only \$0.50.

To generalize again, *a demand curve tells us the marginal value of each unit of the good*. In other words, it tells us the value of each additional—marginal—unit to the next most willing buyer.

Demand versus Quantity Demanded

Here comes a subtle distinction that is crucial to thinking clearly about demand, the distinction between demand and quantity demanded. (The same kind of distinction needs to be made about supply, as we'll see.) Let's approach it with our example: What is the quantity that would be demanded in our little market at a price of, say, $7.50? Only two bottles, because only Charlie and Ellie are each willing to pay that much for a first bottle (they must be very thirsty). What would be the quantity demanded at a price of, say, $2.50? It's eight (two each for Charlie, Ellie, Betsy, and Donna). As these examples illustrate, for any given demand, *quantity demanded* depends on the price: as price increases, quantity demanded decreases, and vice versa.

Now think sharply, remembering that *demand* is the whole set of relationships between prices and quantities, the whole jagged line, the whole "curve": what happens to *demand* (not quantity demanded) when the price falls from $7.50 to $2.50? Answer: nothing. Demand is unchanged. The line does not move. When only price changes, we move northwest or southeast along a stationary demand curve.

But demand itself can also change. In real-world markets, it does so constantly for reasons we'll specify shortly. On a graph, a change in demand means the whole curve moves. For instance, suppose in our example, two new people, Frank and Gary, come to the Little League game. If Frank would pay $11 for a first bottle of water and $6 for a second, whereas

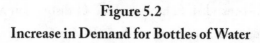

Figure 5.2
Increase in Demand for Bottles of Water

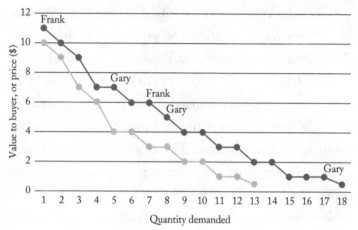

Gary would pay $7 for a first bottle, $5 for a second, and $1 for a third, their desires for water would increase the demand in the market. Adding their demand to the graph would shift the curve up and to the right as shown in Figure 5.2.

We say of a case like this that *demand* has increased.

The Meaning of a Change in Demand

What does a change in *demand* mean about *quantity demanded*, which, you recall, is meaningful only at some price? It means that quantity demanded has increased at every price. To think that way is to think of the increase in demand as a *rightward* shift of the curve. At every dollar amount, the new curve is to the right of the old; at every possible price, a larger amount would be purchased than before.

It is equally valid to think of the increase in demand as an *upward* shift of the curve: when the curve shifts upward in the value (or price) dimension, what has increased? The marginal value has increased; that is, the value of each additional bottle of water has increased.

Of course, the opposite holds for a decrease in demand.

Depending on the problem or situation you are considering, it may be helpful to think of a change in demand as a right shift or left shift or as an up shift or down shift. It you are more interested in what happens to quantities, think right or left; if you are more interested in values, think up or down.

Factors That Change Demand

Here is a quick list of the kinds of changes that can cause a whole demand curve to shift, with an example and quick explanation. Demand shifts because of changes in the following:

- **Demographic patterns.** The aging of baby boomers like me will cause an increased demand for assisted-living facilities, though I hate to think about it.

- **Tastes and preferences.** In the United States at least, a dramatic decrease in the popularity of smoking cigarettes has decreased demand for tobacco.

- **Prices of substitute goods.** If for some reason the price of Coca-Cola were to increase substantially, we would expect an increase in demand for Pepsi, a substitute.

- **Prices of complementary goods.** If the price of peanut butter were to decrease substantially, what would happen to the demand for jelly, which complements peanut butter in sandwiches? With peanut butter less expensive, people would buy more of it, and therefore they would increase their demand for jelly, which goes so well with peanut butter.

- **Expectations of price changes.** If the users of a good or service expect its price to rise in the near future, they will want to buy what they need now, before its price rises, thereby increasing current demand.

- **Demand for goods produced using the good in question.** This type of demand is known as "derived demand." If the demand for housing increases, for example, the demand for two-by-fours will increase as a result. The increased demand for two-by-fours is derived from the increased demand for housing.

6

Supply

Other things remaining equal, will sellers of a good or service want to sell more when they can get high prices for their product or when they can get only low prices for it?

Of course, they will want to sell more at higher prices than at lower prices. This straightforward insight is the *law of supply*. It holds that *greater quantities of a good will be offered for sale at higher prices than at lower prices*, all else equal. It is the logical inverse of the law of demand. Whereas buyers would buy more at lower prices, sellers would sell more at higher prices.

We use "supply" to refer to the actual and potential sellers in a particular market and the prices they would be willing to accept.

What determines the price each different seller would be willing to accept if she had to? It is her opportunity cost of selling. If the price a seller can receive exceeds the value of what she must give up to bring a quantity of the good to market, then she'll be willing to do so; otherwise not.

Consider corn. Different farmers have land with different kinds of soils that are better or worse for growing corn. Some farms get adequate rainfall; others require irrigation. Different farms are closer to or farther from the markets, meaning higher or lower transportation costs. Some farmers manage and maintain their fields and equipment better than others. For these and other reasons, it costs some farmers more than it costs others to bring corn to market. Also, any individual farmer will generally face higher costs for bringing additional quantities of corn to market, because he must grow additional quantities on his marginal fields that require more resources, such as fertilizer or irrigation, to produce a given amount.

Again, let's construct a simple example to illustrate. Imagine a farmer—call him Hiram—who can produce an initial 100 bushels of corn, using his best fields, at a cost of just $4 a bushel. That cost is just the value of his time on the tractor, planting and reaping, because his best fields are so productive he needs no fertilizer or irrigation. He just plants, lets nature do its work, and reaps abundantly. A second 100 bushels, however, he must grow on a field with soil that needs fertilizer, so it costs him $5 a bushel to produce them. And a third 100 bushels—if he produces them at all—would cost him $9 a bushel to produce, because he would have to produce them on his lowest-yielding fields, which require a lot of tilling, fertilizer, and irrigation.

Hiram's neighbors, similarly, are able to produce different quantities of corn by putting different quantities of their land into cultivation and expending different quantities of their time, fertilizer, and irrigation on it to bring forth corn. Suppose these costs of production mean that the different farmers are willing and able to bring corn to market as shown in Table 6.1.

Table 6.1. Cost of Production

Farmer	Cost of producing—lowest price each is willing to accept
Hiram	$4 for the first 100 bushels, $5 for the second, $9 for the third
Irving	$3 for the first 100 bushels, $5 for the second, $6 for the third
Jonas	$4 for the first 100 bushels, $7 for the second, $11 for the third
Kurt	$6 for the first 100 bushels, $8 for the second, $12 for the third

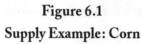

Figure 6.1
Supply Example: Corn

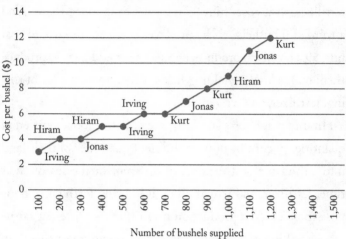

Number of bushels supplied

Just as economists organize the many different (potential) buyers of a good in our imaginations by lining them up according to willingness to pay, we organize the many different (potential) sellers of a good by lining them up in our imaginations according to how little they would be willing to accept for one more unit of the good. That is to say, we line them up according to their costs of production (Figure 6.1).

Notice that here again, as with demand, we put values on the vertical axis—in this case, it's opportunity costs, which are the values of the best alternatives forgone when this corn is produced—and we put quantities on the horizontal axis. (Again, the quantities meant are implicitly for some period of time, perhaps a year in this example.)

This arrangement we call a supply "curve." Notice how it reflects the law of supply: at higher prices, more corn would be offered for sale. Almost never will a supply curve identify the supplier of each quantity of a good by name, as here; almost always, the supply curves we'll consider represent too many suppliers to name in a smoothly upward-sloping line. We present supply this way as we introduce it to emphasize that every point on a supply curve always represents some particular person (or company) willing to accept some particular amount (or more, but not less) for an additional quantity of the good or service.

The Information a Supply Curve Provides

Similar to a demand curve, a supply curve gives us quantity information about costs and cost information about quantities. For example, what does the supply curve for corn in Figure 6.1 tell us about a seller cost of $6 per bushel? It tells us that in this market, 700 bushels can be offered at a cost of $6 per bushel or less. In other words, it tells us that at a price of $6 per bushel, the quantity supplied would be 700 bushels.

At a seller cost of $5 or less, only 500 bushels can be produced, so at a price of $5 per bushel, only 500 would be supplied.

To generalize, a supply curve tells us the quantity supplied at any given price or cost, the quantity that suppliers in that market would be willing and able to sell at that price.

What does a supply curve tell us about any quantity that might be brought to market? It tells us the cost of doing so. For example, what is the cost of offering, say, the 800th bushel of corn in our imaginary market? Trace upward from 800 on the quantity axis until you reach the supply curve. You reach it at the $7 level. Hence, the cost of producing that 800th bushel—to Jonas, in the example—is $7's worth of his land, time, and fertilizer. What's the cost of producing the 1,000th bushel? It's $9: the $9's worth of Hiram's time, fertilizer, irrigation, and land needed to produce it.

Here's a good time for a reminder about the meaning of cost. All costs are best understood as opportunity costs. The cost of producing that 1,000th bushel is the value of the most valuable good(s) that could have been produced instead, using the farmer's time, fertilizer, irrigation, and land that he uses to produce that bushel of corn. To generalize, a supply curve tells us the marginal cost—the cost to its seller of providing each additional unit of the good for sale.

Supply versus Quantity Supplied

Now let's distinguish supply and quantity supplied. Be alert to the difference! What's the quantity supplied in our corn market at a price of $3? It is 100 bushels. At a price of $9? It is 1,000 bushels. Notice that *quantity supplied* depends on price (or cost)—it makes sense to ask about what is the quantity supplied only *at some price*.

Now be alert. What happens to *supply* when the price rises from $3 to $9?

Nothing. Supply does not change. The curve does not move. As price rises from $3 to $9, quantity supplied increases from 100 to 1,000 along a stationary supply curve.

Of course, supply can and does change, all the time, as numbers of producers and costs of production change. On a graph, a change in supply is represented by a movement of the whole curve. For instance, suppose in our example another farmer—let's call him Lawrence—decides to produce corn this season instead of, say, soybeans. Lawrence can produce his first 100 bushels for $1 each, his second 100 bushels for $2 each, and his third for $6 each. Adding Lawrence's supply to that of his neighbors shifts the whole supply curve as shown in Figure 6.2. We say that supply has increased.

Figure 6.2
Increase in Supply of Corn

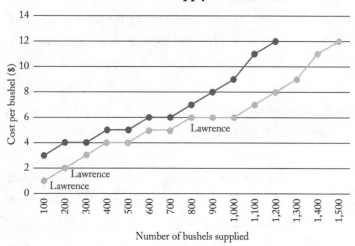

Number of bushels supplied

The Meaning of a Change in Supply

As with demand, a change in supply can be interpreted in two ways. First, it can be thought of as an increase in quantity supplied at every price. In our example, with Lawrence now producing corn also, the quantity supplied at a price of $4 is no longer 300 bushels but 500. At a price of $8, the quantity supplied has increased from 900 to 1,200. Looking at a change in supply this way—starting with price and considering what happens to quantity supplied at that price—is to think about shifts to the right or left.

It is equally valid, and sometimes more useful, to think of a shift in supply as upward or downward. In our example, the supply curve for corn has shifted downward in consequence of Lawrence's production. What decrease does that downward shift signify? Consider the curve at the 1,000th bushel. It was at $9; now it is at $6. What, about the 1,000th bushel, has decreased from $9 to $6? Its cost of production has decreased. That 1,000th bushel now comes from a field where it costs only $6 to produce, instead of from one where it would have cost $9 to produce. In general, then, *an increase in supply signifies a decrease in marginal cost*, the cost of producing each additional quantity.

Of course, the opposite holds for a decrease in supply: represented by a shift of the curve upward and left, it signifies an increase in marginal cost. As with demand, it is useful to think about changes in supply as either right or left shifts or up or down shifts, depending on whether we are focused on changes in quantities or changes in costs.

Factors That Can Change Supply

Various factors can change supply—cause the whole supply curve to shift. The most important are changes in the following:

- **Number of suppliers.** This factor is straightforward; more suppliers mean greater supply, and vice versa.

- **Input prices.** A change in the price of a resource used to produce a good will change the supply of that good by making it more or less costly to produce. For example, an increase in the price of fertilizer would decrease the supply of corn by making it more costly to produce corn on land that needs fertilizer.

- **Technology.** In our era, nothing is doing so much to increase the supply of goods as improvements in technology, in the tools and techniques used to produce. Electronics provide the clearest example, as improvements in technology steadily drive down the cost and increase the availability of computers, smartphones, and all sorts of other devices.

7

Price Determination: Demand and Supply Together

Now that we have considered what demand and supply mean, let's see how their interaction determines market prices and quantities exchanged.

In any market, there is a strong tendency for the going price to approximate the theoretical *equilibrium price*, also known as the "market-clearing" price. In a supply-and-demand graph, that's the price at the intersection of the supply curve and demand curve. Correspondingly, there is a strong tendency for the quantity of the good or service exchanged in a period to approximate the *equilibrium quantity*. In a standard graph,

Figure 7.1
Market Equilibrium

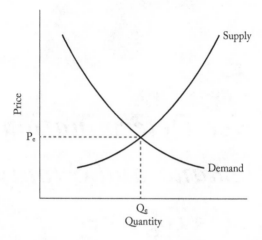

that's the quantity at the intersection of the supply curve and demand curve (Figure 7.1).

Why is that price (P_e) called the "equilibrium" price? What is equal there? To see, trace along that price level to the demand curve and down from there to the quantity axis to find the quantity demanded. Mark it on the quantity axis. Then trace along that same price level to the supply curve and down again to the quantity axis to find the quantity supplied. Mark it also. Aha! At that price, and only at that price, are quantity demanded and quantity supplied equal, "in equilibrium."

But that's not the only equality at that intersection of the supply curve and demand curve. Trace up from the equilibrium quantity (Q_e) to the demand curve to find the value to its buyer of that last unit that would be purchased at that price, the "marginal value." Then trace up from that equilibrium quantity to the supply curve to find the value of the resources used to make that last unit available on the market, its "marginal cost." Aha again! For the last unit that would change hands at the equilibrium price, and that unit only, its marginal value (to the buyer) equals its marginal cost (to the seller).

The theoretical equilibrium price is also known as the *market-clearing price* because at that price (alone), no disappointed buyers or sellers are left in the market. Every buyer is able to buy as much as he is willing to buy at that price, and every seller is able to sell as much as she is willing to sell at that price.

Now—and this is crucial to understanding the market process—*why* do the actual prices on a market so reliably stay close to this theoretical equilibrium price? (They really do.) The reason is that as buyers and sellers follow their own personal incentives to do the best they can for themselves, they naturally push the market price toward the equilibrium or market-clearing level. Let's see why.

In a world of scarcity, buyers must compete with other buyers for scarce goods and services, and sellers must compete with other sellers for customers. A particular price at a particular time results from competition among buyers and among sellers. Competing bids from would-be buyers push the price upward; competing offers from would-be sellers push the price downward. Each would-be buyer bases his bids on his particular knowledge of the value of the good to him. In a kind of implicit auction, he bids as little as he can while still remaining in the running, and he never bids more than the good's value to him. At the same time, each would-be seller bases her offers to sell on her own particular knowledge of her costs—what she must give up to provide the good for sale. She asks as high a price as she can while still remaining in the running, and she never asks a price lower than what it costs her to offer the good for sale.

Out of that ongoing competitive process of bids and offers emerges the ever-fluctuating market price of the good.

With regard to a simple example shown in a standard supply-and-demand graph (Figure 7.2), suppose supply increases for some reason—perhaps a new seller has gone into business—so that the $8 price currently asked in the market is higher than the new market-clearing price ($6).

Figure 7.2
Change Due to an Increase in Supply

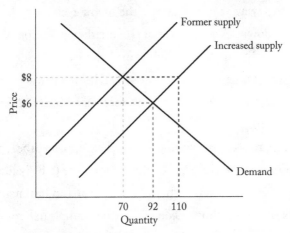

At $8, sellers would now want to sell 110 units of the good per period, while buyers would want to buy only 70. Some of those sellers—particularly those well down and left on the curve because their costs of providing the good are low—will undercut that too-high price of $8, and their competitors will have to lower *their* prices in response.

At the same time, would-be buyers who find the current price too high hold off buying. Some might actually coun-teroffer with a lower price. Others wait for the good to go on sale, or they do more comparison shopping, looking for a lower price. Sellers soon see that they must reduce their asking price to win these customers.

In this way, a price above the market-clearing level is pushed down. And the actions of market participants will tend to keep pushing it down until the market clears, at a price where everyone can buy or sell all he or she wants at that new equilibrium price (in the example, a quantity of 92 at a price of $6).

The process is similar—but headed in the other direction—when the price happens for a time to be below the market-clearing level, perhaps because demand has increased from a rise in consumer incomes. See the example in Figure 7.3.

At the now-too-low old price of $200, the buyers would like to buy twice as much as sellers are willing to sell. Suppliers would run out; buyers would be disappointed. In very short order, alert sellers would realize that they can charge more and still sell their inventory. Disappointed buyers might offer a higher price for first access to the next shipment of the good. In such ways, the price is pushed up, and it keeps getting pushed up until the new market-clearing price is reached ($300 in the example). At that point—until conditions change again—no one has an incentive to ask or offer a different price, because all can buy or sell as much as they want at that price.

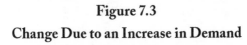

Figure 7.3
Change Due to an Increase in Demand

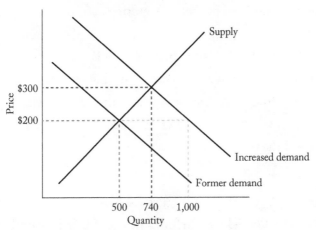

This is the process of price determination by the interplay of supply and demand. Notice that nobody unilaterally *sets* the market price; it *emerges* out of the interaction of many individuals. In economist Antony Davies's useful phrase, "Prices are metrics that reflect value, not levers that set value."

When Supply or Demand Changes

Now we have all we need to understand how a change in either supply or demand will cause a change in both the market price and the quantity of a good bought and sold in a period of time.

Consider the market for, say, natural gas, which has been transformed in recent years. Improved technologies of horizontal drilling and hydraulic fracturing have allowed the production of vast quantities of natural gas (and oil) from shale deep in the earth's crust. In other words, they have greatly increased the supply of natural gas. Figure 7.4 represents the natural gas market before and after those technological improvements and shows why market participants have lowered the price.

Figure 7.4
Natural Gas Market before and after Shale Revolution

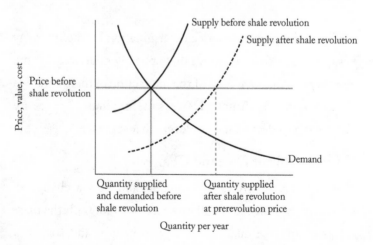

The quantity of gas that suppliers would like to sell at the old price, now that the shale revolution has occurred, exceeds the quantity buyers are willing to buy at the old price (Figure 7.5). To induce buyers to buy more, sellers with costs below that old price offer to sell for less. Their competitors have to match those price cuts. At the same time, alert demanders, noticing the increased supply, shop around for lower prices.

Figure 7.5
Natural Gas Market after Shale Revolution

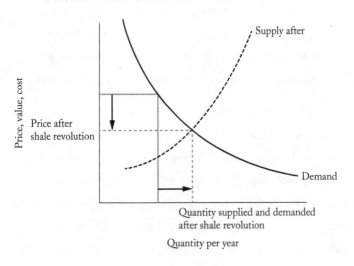

This competitive pushing down of prices continues as long as the price is above the new market-clearing level and quantity supplied is greater than quantity demanded. Very quickly, this competition drives the price down to the new, post-shale-revolution level at which quantity supplied once again equals quantity demanded. The quantity of gas changing hands in a given period increases, because buyers buy more at a lower price.

For an example of how price and quantity change in response to a change in demand, consider the market for apartments to rent. Suppose that, as reported by CBS News in July 2013:

> Buying a home is getting more expensive and more difficult. With mortgage rates and home prices rising, and with mortgage lenders still demanding high down payments and pristine credit scores to get a loan, more potential homebuyers are content to rent.[3]

How will that affect the rental price of an apartment?

Figure 7.6 shows why market participants will surely raise the monthly rental rates. At the old rate, the number of apartments people would like to rent is greater than the number offered for rent. On the supply side, landlords—besieged by people asking them if they have any vacancies—would see that they could raise rates once their current leases expire and quickly rerent those apartments. On the demand side,

Figure 7.6
Rental Apartment Market before and after Buying a Home Gets More Expensive

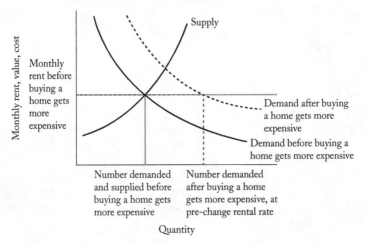

Monthly rent, value, cost

Supply

Monthly rent before buying a home gets more expensive

Demand after buying a home gets more expensive

Demand before buying a home gets more expensive

Number demanded and supplied before buying a home gets more expensive

Number demanded after buying a home gets more expensive, at pre-change rental rate

Quantity

people eager to rent an apartment would compete for those that become available by offering more than the current rent.

This bidding up of rental rates would continue until the new market-clearing (or equilibrium) rental level is reached, at the intersection of the supply curve and the new demand curve (Figure 7.7). That's the monthly rental rate at which the number of apartments that tenants would like to occupy equals the number of apartments that their owners make

Figure 7.7
Rental Apartment Market After Buying a Home Gets More Expensive

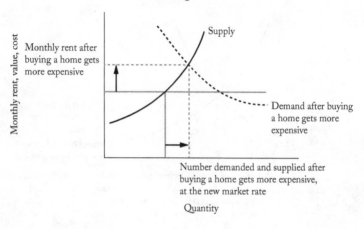

available ("quantity demanded equals quantity supplied"). And at that rental rate, the value to the tenant of the last apartment rented equals the cost to the landlord of making it available to rent.

What's Missing from Supply-and-Demand Graphs?

It's important to keep in mind the limitations of supply-and-demand analysis. It is a robust tool of thought, but it is only that—a tool of thought—a way of organizing and simplifying in our minds the tremendous complexity and variety of real markets so that we can think clearly about the relationships among buyers' values, sellers' costs, prices, and quantities. Think how many other characteristics of real markets supply-and-demand graphs ignore: hours of operation, friendliness of salespeople, availability of parking, location, packaging, availability of financing or free shipping, and many others. A supply-and-demand graph is to a market as a stick figure is to a human being. Essentials are represented, but most of what makes particular markets and human beings interesting is ignored.

And Then What Happens?

One of the important limitations of supply-and-demand graphs is that they can represent only a point or period in time. In reality, time does not stop, change is incessant, and people respond to a situation at one moment in ways that will change it in the next.

Consequently, an essential practice of good economic thinking is constantly to ask, "And then what happens?" When supply or demand changes in a market, so that the going price rises or falls, the world does not stop once the price in that market rises or falls to the new market-clearing level. The reason is that changing prices change incentives. The moment a price begins to move in response to a change in demand or supply, that price movement alters the incentives for people in the market and starts to change their behavior accordingly. People are constantly responding to conditions and opportunities and using their ingenuity to create and take advantage of new opportunities offered by changed prices, so markets never come to a state of rest.

For example, consider again the natural gas market we discussed earlier. One large category of natural gas buyers is electrical power-generating companies. The steam that turns their generators can be created by burning coal, oil, or natural gas. As natural gas has become much less expensive, power companies that are replacing their coal- and oil-burning plants are replacing them with plants that burn now relatively cheaper (and cleaner-burning) natural gas. As this conversion proceeds, more plants will need natural gas; hence, demand for natural gas will increase. This demand-side response to lower prices will tend to push the price of natural gas back upward.

At the same time, think what incentive the now-lower price of natural gas gives suppliers of natural gas. Are they more or less willing than before to invest millions of dollars in exploring for new shale deposits and digging new wells, now that the price is lower than before? They are less willing, of course. In consequence, as I write this book (summer 2015), fewer new wells are being drilled than when prices were higher. Many partially completed wells have been mothballed, waiting for higher prices to make completing them profitable again.

Accordingly, supply is not increasing as fast as it was, so there is less downward pressure on prices than a few months ago.

As you analyze price changes using supply and demand, remember that those curves represent people, flesh-and-blood buyers (demand) and sellers (supply), and people are constantly learning, reacting, and innovating. Never treat a supply-and-demand graph as showing the end of the story. It's just an episode at best. Look at it and ask, "And then what happens?"

That's the end of our quick look at how supply and demand can help us think about the behavior of prices in a free market. But why should we even care about prices? We should because they tell us all what to do to keep our actions coordinated with the actions of others. To that essential function we turn next.

Part Three:

Free Markets

Now we turn to why markets should be free. The freer the markets we live in—the more complete the security of our property and the more freedom we have to engage in voluntary, peaceful exchange—the more fully we people can flourish.

Free-market prices are necessary to communicate the dispersed knowledge we need to coordinate our various actions. Free-market profit and loss are necessary to guide entrepreneurs' discovery of how to create value for other people. Private ownership and freedom of exchange are necessary to give everyone the incentive to serve other people as they pursue their own purposes.

8

Prices and Knowledge

Prices are precious. Free-market prices that emerge from the voluntary interaction of buyers and sellers are necessary to human well-being. Few lessons in economics are more important than this.

The economy is a fantastically complex, worldwide system of human cooperation. We all pursue our own purposes, no one is in charge of the whole system, and yet we cooperate. We all cooperate daily with countless people we don't know, but whose particular knowledge of ever-changing circumstances we must somehow take into account in order to coordinate our actions with theirs. Prices make this knowledge available and this cooperation possible.

We need free markets because we need the information that free-market prices give us about what others know. We have no other way to communicate this information to all who might use it. This is the first of three principles of spontaneous economic order that account for why human beings need free markets:

> *Market prices coordinate the actions of billions pursuing their myriad goals, by communicating the changing, particular knowledge of everyone about the availability and potential uses of everything.*

This chapter explores that principle. It looks at how free-market prices coordinate all our different plans and how government interference with prices causes trouble.

Three Lessons and a Question from "I, Pencil"

To appreciate the all-important role of prices in the economy—indeed, in society generally—a good place to start is Leonard Read's classic 1958 article, "I, Pencil." I recommend that readers who have not yet read this delightful piece download it from the Internet and read it along with this lesson. (A complete version is available from the Library of Economics and Liberty at http://www.econlib.org/library/Essays/rdPncl1.html.)

The narrator in the essay, "a lead pencil—the ordinary wooden pencil familiar to all boys and girls and adults who can read and write," asserts at the outset that, despite his seeming simplicity, "not a single person on the face of this earth knows how to make me." To back up that astonishing statement, the pencil describes his "family tree," the various and far-flung processes required to produce the many inputs that become a pencil: cedar wood, tint, graphite lead, lacquer, the brass ferrule, the eraser. The number of different skills that go into making the many elements of a high-quality modern pencil is really astonishing. Here are just a few of them:

- Logging, to produce the cedar wood

- Mining graphite for the "lead"

- Mining zinc and copper from which to make the brass ferrule that joins the main pencil with the eraser

- Milling the cedar logs into pencil-length slats

- Making the machines that tint the slats and wax the slats

- Operating those machines

- Making the kilns for drying the slats once they are tinted and waxed

- Operating those kilns

- Making chemicals, including ammonium hydroxide, sulfonated tallow, candelilla wax, paraffin wax, hydrogenated natural fats, cadmium sulfide, castor oil, resins, carbon black, factice, and vulcanizing agents

- Refining and combining zinc and copper into brass

After describing all these processes, the pencil asks, "Does anyone wish to challenge my earlier assertion that no single person on the face of this earth knows how to make me?" Probably not; not if knowing how means knowing deeply enough to be actually able to do it. It's not credible that any one person could do the logging, the mining, the milling, the chemistry, and the metallurgy involved, not to mention making all the related equipment necessary. The pencil says:

> There isn't a single person in all these millions, including the president of the pencil company, who contributes more than a tiny, infinitesimal bit of know-how. From the standpoint of know-how the only difference between the miner of graphite in Ceylon and the logger in Oregon is in the type of know-how. Neither the miner nor the logger can be dispensed with, any more than can the chemist at the factory or the worker in the oil field—paraffin being a by-product of petroleum.

Here is the first of three fundamental lessons about economic life that "I, Pencil" teaches: The human knowledge that is essential for producing the things we want and need is fantastically dispersed around the world. It is in the heads and hands of thousands—or millions—of people. There is so much knowledge in these processes that no one person or group could possibly know more than a tiny fraction of it.

The second lesson is that all who participate are self-interested. They are not selfish in the pejorative sense, but self-interested:

> Neither the worker in the oil field nor the chemist nor the digger of graphite or clay nor any who mans or makes the ships or trains or trucks nor the one who runs the machine that does the knurling on my bit of metal nor the president of the company performs his singular task because he wants me. Each one wants me less, perhaps, than does a child in the first grade. Indeed, there are some among this vast multitude who never saw a pencil nor would they know how to use one. Their motivation is other than me. Perhaps it is something like this: Each of these millions sees that he can thus exchange his tiny know-how for the goods and services he needs or wants. I may or may not be among these items.

The third lesson is

> a fact still more astounding: The absence of a master mind, of anyone dictating or forcibly directing these countless actions which bring me into being. No trace of such a person can be found. Instead, we find the Invisible Hand at work.

No one is in charge. There is no mastermind, no boss. In a very real sense, the process is *out of control*. People work together to produce pencils and printers and sewing machines and smartphones, but nobody manages their production from start to finish. Nobody could manage these processes as a whole, because they are too complex for any person or group even to begin to grasp, much less direct. Indeed, where people have tried to direct production processes, as in the old Soviet Union, they have failed utterly. Production must happen spontaneously—without central direction—if it is to go forward smoothly.

A market economy is a *spontaneous order*; its orderliness and coherence happen, without any design or plan, in response to the behavior of its constituent parts. Language is like this—it was not invented or designed; rather, language evolves out of the interactions of people seeking to communicate. Snowflakes are spontaneous orders. They are beautiful, even perfect in their way, but not designed. They happen as a consequence of the interaction of water molecules under certain conditions of air pressure, temperature and humidity. The Internet is a spontaneous, undesigned order that is constantly evolving in response to human desires and innovation.

Together, these three lessons about the economy raise the key question for this section:

If

(a) the knowledge necessary for production is spread all over the globe, and

(b) everybody whose knowledge and skills we need is self-interested, and

(c) nobody is in charge,

then

how can it all work so smoothly and dependably?

It would seem to be a recipe for chaos! *What provides the coordination that keeps a decentralized market economy running so smoothly and productively?*

We take the coordination for granted: Is there any one of us who doubts that if we wanted a pencil today, we could go to the university store or the local drugstore and find one? Of

course not—we would be surprised if there were not a supply of pencils there. But how does it come to be that pencils
are for sale, in about the right quantities, in lots of stores all
around (the commercialized part of) the world—with no one
in charge of getting them there?

Consider the wood of the cedar trees that goes into the
pencils: Why do the lumber companies cut about the right
amount of cedar, rather than too much oak or maple instead?
Once the cedar is harvested, it has many different uses. My
wife has equipped our closets with cedar hangers; our back-
yard fence is cedar; some picnic tables are cedar. Why doesn't
too much cedar go to fencing and picnic tables and too little
go to hangers and pencils?

There is perhaps no more important insight in all of economics than the answer to this question: *what provides the
coordination* among the millions of people who contribute
directly or indirectly to the making of pencils and every other
good or service?

Prices do. When pencil companies need more cedar for
pencils and so bid up the price of cedar relative to that of
oak, lumber companies harvest more cedar and less oak. The
higher price of cedar makes cedar fences and picnic tables
more expensive, so fence and table buyers purchase fewer
cedar fences and tables and more of other varieties instead.

Market prices thus function as a vast telecommunications system, signaling to everyone the relative availability and urgency of need for different goods and thereby telling us how to keep our production and use of goods adjusted to the wants and actions of others. This is the principle I mentioned earlier:

> *Market prices coordinate the actions of billions pursuing their myriad goals, by communicating the changing, particular knowledge of everyone about the availability and potential uses of everything.*

Market prices are therefore strictly necessary to allow societies to function smoothly and productively. Without market prices—not just any prices set arbitrarily but prices determined in free exchange—human society would regress to savagery, because we would not know how to use our scarce resources sensibly. Prices provide us with essential information about the current and anticipated state of things in society, as understood by everyone involved. They give us a reliable estimate of the value of one more of any good and the cost of making it available. They communicate concisely, to everyone interested, the specialized knowledge that is spread all over society. Prices need never be exactly "right" to do their job well; in fact, most prices are to some degree "wrong" most of the time because they reflect people's mistakes, misjudgments, and misinformation, as well as their good judgments and sound information. Nevertheless, market prices do a marvelous job for us, and nothing else can take their place.

A good way to understand how prices communicate dispersed knowledge is to consider what a fix we would be in if we had no prices. Let's consider such a situation with a thought experiment.

A Railroad Thought Experiment

Imagine yourself the commissar of railroads in the old Soviet Union. It is the early days after the revolution of 1917; you and your comrades are trying to eliminate markets and money relations, to do away with the anarchy of markets, and to plan directly for the good of the people. Suppose you are truly dedicated to your task, as many of the Bolsheviks were—they worked long days for little pay, burning with desire to make communism work. You are not out to line your own pockets; you are genuinely striving to do what is best for the Soviet Union.

Now suppose you want to build a railroad line connecting City A to City B. Between the two cities stands a mountain range that presents you with a choice: you may build the railroad either through the mountains or around them.

Both choices have advantages and disadvantages. If you go through the mountains, you will save greatly on the amount of steel you use, because that route would be much shorter than going around. At the same time, however, going through the mountains will require a great deal of engineering to design the bridges, tunnels, and elaborate grading necessary to get the railroad through the mountains. By contrast, if you go around the mountains, you will need to use very little engineering because the line can be laid out simply on level ground. But you will have to lay much more steel rail because the route is longer.

Which route would you choose? Would you go through the mountains, saving on steel but consuming more engineering? Or would you go around the mountains, to save on engineering while consuming more steel? You are the commissar of railroads, and the choice is entirely yours. Remember, we assume that you care only about what is best for the nation as a whole. Which would you choose?

To keep the thought experiment simple, let us ignore all considerations other than the consumption of engineering and steel. Of course, there are also the ties and gravel, explosives and excavating equipment, labor of many sorts, fuel, machinery, and so on. Let us ignore them or assume that the same amounts would be needed on both routes.

Once the railroad is built, each route has different advantages. For example, the route through the mountains would be shorter and hence would provide a quicker trip between the cities. On the other hand, going around the mountains would allow the road to serve more towns and farms and factories along the way. Again, let us ignore all these considerations, or assume that they come out even, so that we have a manageable problem to think about: use more steel and less engineering, or the other way around?

How would you decide?

Consider the kind of information you would need to take into account. You know that there are pressing needs for steel all around the country. Steel is needed to make girders for new hospitals, pots and pans, vehicles of all descriptions, surgical instruments, and thousands of other valuable goods. If you use more steel on your railroad line, less steel will be available for all those other important uses.

At the same time, engineering services are urgently needed all around the country. Engineers' time and expertise are needed to design and build irrigation systems, mines, harbor installations, and thousands of other systems that will improve the country's productivity. If you use a great deal of engineering in building your railroad, the country will wait precious months for those other systems and their services.

So there is your problem: If, when you build your railroad line, the alternative uses of steel—the girders, pots and pans, vehicles, surgical instruments, and so on—are more important and pressing to the nation than the systems and services that need engineering, then you should put the engineers to work building the railroad through the mountains. That way, you would save on the relatively more scarce and precious steel and use more of the relatively abundant engineering. But if the other uses of engineering—the irrigation systems, mines, harbor installations, and the like—are more important and pressing than the other uses of steel, then you should run the line around the mountains to save on the relatively scarce and important engineering services and use more of the relatively abundant steel.

What would you decide?

* * * * *

When I ask this question in lectures, most of my audience have no answer. And that's the right answer.

Think how much you would need to know in order make the judgment: In order to know the value of steel in other uses, you would need detailed information on the value of the uses to which it would be put. Consider a new hospital that might be built with new steel girders. What is its value? To answer that question, you would need to know what the various doctors, nurses, and hospital administrators know about currently available hospitals, their state of repair, the benefits of the new location and increased space, and so on. To know the value of steel in making pots and pans, you would need to know what various householders and restaurateurs know about the condition of their existing pans, their expectations of need for more pans or pans of different sizes, their preferences for steel pots and pans as opposed to copper, and so on. You would need similar kinds of knowledge to assess the value of steel for manufacturing different kinds of cars and trucks.

Think how dispersed and interconnected the information is that you would need with respect to even one vehicle. To know the value of, say, a new truck, you would need to know what the trucker knows about the value of the larger or faster shipments he could make with the new truck. To know the value of particular shipments, however, say, of produce to grocery stores in the region, you would need to know what the grocer knows about the value of fresh groceries on his shelves. To know that, you would need to know what the customers know about the value of those groceries in making their families' dinners.

The same kinds of considerations hold on the engineering side. What would you need to know in order to assess the value of engineering used to construct, say, an irrigation system? You would need to know what the farmers know about how much the yield of their fields would increase with irrigation. But to know the value of that increased yield, the farmers need somehow to know what their consumers know about the value to them of the additional food produced.

In short, to make a sound assessment of whether steel or engineering is more important in other uses, and accordingly whether to build your railroad line through or around the mountains, you would need an overwhelming amount of detailed knowledge held by thousands, nay, millions of people throughout your society, about the values of all the different uses to which steel and engineering could be put. How would you get that information? Would you send out surveys? As commissar, you hold absolute power; you may execute anyone who does not tell you promptly what you ask.

But do people even know what they prefer until they are faced with an actual choice? Often they don't, so they might not even be able to answer survey questions accurately. And how would you aggregate all this information, if you could get it all? Isn't it clear that you simply *could not get the information you need*?

Furthermore, even if you could get complete and timely information about what everyone knows that's relevant to the use of steel and engineering, you would still need to deduce from it where to build your railroad. How could you possibly know what all that information means for your decision? How would you begin to make sense of it?

If you could not say which route you would choose for the railroad from City A to City B, you gave the right answer. It is impossible to decide on any rational basis. In the words of Ludwig von Mises, who first pointed out this problem to the socialists, you would be "groping in the dark." You would have to guess. Even though you have absolute power as commissar of railroads, and even though you have the best will in the world and a burning desire to make communism outperform capitalism, you would be unable to determine the best route, because you could not possibly know which route would be less costly to society overall. The knowledge you would need is too vast, too dispersed, too specialized, and too changeable.

This is the *knowledge problem of central planning*. It explains why comprehensive socialism must necessarily fail, even if those involved have the best intentions: central planners cannot get the knowledge they need in order to plan effectively.

* * * * *

Now let's change the thought experiment slightly. Instead of commissar of railroads in the old Soviet Union, you are now the chief operating officer of a for-profit railroad company, somewhere in the capitalist West. You face the same problem. You want to run a railroad line from City C to City D, and a mountain range stands between them, so you must go either through or around. How would you decide on your route? Again, assume that all the other costs and benefits come out the same on both routes, so that the only variables to consider are the different amounts of steel and engineering you would use. What would you do?

Unless you are quite unusual, you would do what's cheapest. You would calculate the total cost of each route, in each case multiplying the amount of steel required by the price of steel and adding that to the amount of engineering required times the price of engineering. Whichever route gives the lower total cost is the one you'd choose.

Typical greedy capitalist! All you care about is the company's profits, the bottom line. Like capitalists the world over, you would give no consideration to the overall good of the nation. You would ignore whether steel or engineering is more valuable in other uses, even though that is crucial to the overall productivity and living standards of your society. You would just do whatever is cheapest, focusing on your company's profits and ignoring the well-being of other people.

But—and here's the marvel—in doing whatever is cheapest in a free economy, you unwittingly *do* take into consideration every single piece of information and every bit of human knowledge about the values of unnumbered alternative uses of steel and engineering. You learn from examining a few numbers all that the central planner would be powerless to find out in months of investigation. And choosing the cheaper route spares the resources that are more valuable in other uses. How? Because all the relevant knowledge available is embodied in the *prices* of steel and engineering. The lower total cost of one route compared with the other tells us that the combined total of steel and engineering needed for the cheaper route is less valuable *in other uses* than the combination needed for the more expensive route.

Suppose many existing hospitals are small and out-of-date (in a free market for hospital care). The stronger the desire for new space, the more health care companies and philanthropists will be willing to pay contractors for the construction of new hospitals; and therefore, the more the contractors will be willing and able to pay, if necessary, for the steel girders with which to build them. The price of steel likewise reflects the number of householders desiring to buy new steel pots and pans and the urgency of their desires. It reflects the amount any trucker will pay for a new delivery truck, which reflects the value of the produce deliveries he makes, which reflects the value of the groceries on the shelves, which reflects the value of the final consumer's dinner. The number and urgency of all these direct and indirect desires for steel are reflected in the price offered for steel, as the various would-be buyers compete for its limited quantity.

The price of engineering at any time is determined in the same manner. If new irrigation systems would improve farm output only a little, then farmers would not be willing to pay much for the engineers' time, and the price of engineering would be correspondingly lower.

This railroad example shows that market prices give us a reliable gauge of the value of goods and services. As we saw in Chapter 7, a market price reflects the value to the last buyer just barely willing to pay that price and the cost to the last seller just barely willing to accept that price. Thus, the market price (at that moment—remember prices constantly fluctuate) is the actual value in society of one more unit of that good at that time—what (someone in) society gives up in providing one more and the benefit (someone in) society realizes from gaining one more.

Only with this knowledge can we calculate the least costly ways of producing the things we want and thereby satisfy as many different human wants as possible. That is one supremely important reason that free-market prices—and hence the free markets they depend on—are so important to human flourishing.

With market prices to guide us, we can make use of the knowledge of everyone in society about the supplies of and uses for every different resource. (One highly recommended further reading on this point is F. A. Hayek's 1945 article, "The Use of Knowledge in Society," available from the Library of Economics and Liberty, http://www.econlib.org /library/Essays/hykKnw1.html.) In George Selgin's useful term, prices serve as "knowledge surrogates."[4] They distill the knowledge of millions of people into a number. With market prices to guide us, each of us can stay well coordinated with all the millions of others, never using for a less important purpose what someone else needs for a more important purpose. Without market prices, however, we would be in trouble, unable to coordinate our innumerable activities. The next chapter illustrates that trouble with some supply-and-demand analysis and offers a memorable story.

9

The Problems with
Price Controls

Consequences of Interfering with Free-Market Pricing

Price controls are pieces of legislation that set either lower limits or upper limits—floors or ceilings—on legally permissible prices. Their purpose is generally to protect some group in society from prices the legislators find to be "too high" or "too low" for some reason. Rent controls, for example, are price ceilings that aim to protect tenants from market-clearing rent levels that are considered "too high." Anti-price-gouging laws (sometimes passed after natural disasters, as we will see) similarly aim to protect buyers from prices that are "too high." Minimum-wage laws are price floors that aim to protect workers from wages that are "too low." Milk price supports are price floors that aim to protect dairy farmers from prices that are "too low."

These legislated restrictions on the free movement of prices all have the unintended consequence of reducing economic coordination. They prevent markets from clearing. Price ceilings cause shortages; price floors cause surpluses. Those shortages and surpluses hurt some of the very people who are supposed to be helped by price controls.

Consider rent controls, for example (Figure 9.1). Suppose in a particular city the market for two-bedroom apartments

Figure 9.1
Example of Rent Control: Market for
Two-Bedroom Apartments

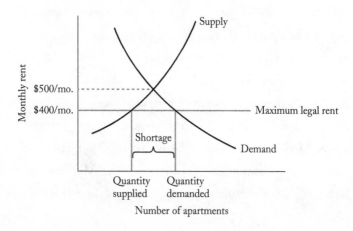

would clear at $500 a month, but rents are restricted to no more than $400 a month. At that rental rate, the number of apartments people would like to rent (the quantity demanded) would exceed the number made available (the quantity supplied). The difference is the magnitude of the shortage of apartments the rent control would cause.

That shortage consists of people who simply cannot find an apartment. Those fortunate enough to have an apartment already are protected from paying $500 a month instead of $400, but those who cannot find an apartment are "protected" from getting the housing they want.

The artificially low rental rate gives discoordinating incentives to both tenants and (potential) landlords. Some people now occupying two-bedroom apartments who don't need that much space—such as couples whose children have moved out—would choose to downsize to a one-bedroom apartment if they had to pay the free-market rate of $500 a month for two bedrooms. Their downsizing would make way for larger families. But the rent control decreases their incentive to do that. On the supply side, the artificially low rental rate decreases the incentive for people to make apartments available, perhaps by constructing new apartment buildings or reconfiguring a three-bedroom house into a two-bedroom apartment for tenants and a one-bedroom apartment for the homeowner.

Figure 9.2
Example of Minimum-Wage Laws' Effects:
Market for Low-Skill Labor Services

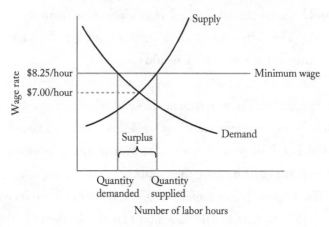

Consider minimum-wage laws (Figure 9.2). Suppose in a particular city the market for low-skilled labor services—such as flipping hamburgers or retrieving shopping carts from grocery store parking lots—would clear at $7.00 an hour, but wages are restricted to no less than $8.25 an hour. At that wage rate, the number of worker hours that employers would like to hire (quantity demanded) would fall short of the number of hours low-skilled workers would like to work (quantity supplied). The difference is the magnitude of the surplus of labor services the minimum-wage law would cause.

That surplus of labor services is what we call unemployment. It consists mostly of young people so poorly educated and ill prepared for the workplace that the work they are able to do creates less value for a business than the wage the business must pay. Businesses would lose money hiring such workers, so they don't hire them at all. Those fortunate enough to hold their low-end jobs are protected from being paid only $7.00 an hour, but those who cannot find a job are "protected" by the minimum-wage law from receiving any wage at all.

The higher wage that employers would be forced to pay low-skill workers, if they hire them at all, gives employers an incentive to invest in technologies that can replace human workers, such as ordering by smartphone or kiosk at fast-food places. Alternatively, employers can keep the same number of employees on the payroll if they offset wage increases by reducing other costly benefits, such as health insurance, on-the-job training, coffee breaks, or flexible hours. Either way, some workers lose.

Minimum-wage laws are harmful on net. They violate freedom of contract. They cause unemployment. They should be abolished. Remember that they are not necessary to hold wages up at the market-clearing level; competition among employers takes care of that. In a free market, employers don't control wages; the competitive market process does.

Any employer who systematically pays more than the going market wage will tend to lose out to competitors who pay only the market wage and therefore can charge a bit less for their product. And any employer who tries to pay less than the going market wage will find herself unable to attract the workers she wants; other employers offering the market wage will bid those workers away from her. Remember Antony Davies's useful insight: prices, including wages, are metrics that reflect values, not levers that set value.

Should Prices Ever Be Controlled?

How far can we push this insistence on the value of market prices? Is it *never* in the public interest for governments to control prices?

Let's seek answers to those questions by considering an extreme case—price gouging after a hurricane. Many people condemn *those* market prices as unjust and support price controls. For example, after Hurricane Hugo hit Charleston, South Carolina, in September 1989, prices of many needed goods shot up. Because the storm surge had polluted the city water system, bottled water was in great demand, rising drastically in price. Because power lines were down all over the city, gasoline-powered generators that had sold for a few hundred dollars before the storm were going for several thousand dollars afterward. Ice that had sold for $1 a bag was selling for $10 a bag.

Should grocers be prevented from raising bottled water prices from, say, $1 a gallon to $10 a gallon? Should hardware store owners be prevented from raising gasoline-powered generator prices from, say, $700 to $7,000? Or is it best for the people of Charleston, generally considered, to let those prices rise, to let the market prices prevail?

In Charleston after Hurricane Hugo, anti-gouging sentiments carried the day politically. The mayor and city council passed legislation making it a crime to sell goods for more than they had sold before the hurricane. The punishment for that crime was up to 30 days in jail and a $200 fine.

Let us leave aside the important philosophical question of whether it is right or wrong to charge such high prices. Let us focus instead on the economic consequences of letting prices rise sky-high versus holding them down to prestorm levels.

Suppose the Charleston politicians had left the markets free and allowed grocers to sell their bottled water at, say, $10 a gallon, up from $1 a gallon. What would that $10 a gallon price have communicated? What would it have "said" to those who first arrived at the stores?

It would have communicated—in the summary form of that shocking $10 per gallon price—the combined knowledge and judgments of many people in and around Charleston as to the extent of damage to the city water system, the amount of bottled water available on store shelves, how long it would probably take to get the system fixed, and how hard it would be to bring new bottled water into the city. To those arriving at the store, the $10 per gallon price would have boiled all this information down to this message: "Clean water is very scarce right now, lots of people want some. Bring it if you have it, and don't take much."

One excellent characteristic of market prices is that at the same time they communicate dispersed knowledge, they provide an incentive to act on that knowledge. In the wonderful phrase from professors Tyler Cowen and Alex Tabarrok, "A price is a signal wrapped up in an incentive."[5] What incentive would the $10 price give buyers arriving at grocery stores, eager to stock up on clean water? It would give them an incentive to buy less, which is exactly the response needed by other people who have not yet had a chance to get to a grocery store. It would give the early arrivals a strong incentive to leave water for the late arrivals. Here again, the market price fosters coordination: while bottled water is precious and scarce, its high price motivates people to share the short supply with others.

By contrast, consider what actually happened in Charleston in 1989 after the price controls were enacted. People who arrived first at the grocery stores bought all the water they could carry, quickly stripping the shelves. When those from harder-hit areas finally arrived, there was no water for them. Market prices were forbidden, so coordination broke down.

Notice how this phenomenon puts the issue of fairness in another light. Observers of the high price might ask themselves *who* would buy water at that price? "The rich," they think, and that seems unfair to people with less money. But if instead we ask *how much* people would buy at that price, the answer is that probably all buyers, rich and poor, would buy less than they otherwise would, and thereby would leave more for others. The prestorm price of $1 a gallon was certainly unfair to those who couldn't get to stores early, because a price of $1 a gallon meant they got no water at all—it was all sold out. Had a high market price been allowed to do its essential job, it would have deterred both rich and poor from buying more than they considered essential and would have spread out the available supply among all the residents of Charleston. In an important way, it would have been much fairer for everyone to have a chance to buy some water at $10 a gallon than for a lucky few to buy up the whole supply at $1 a gallon.

What happened when price controls were put into place is really worse than what we have described so far, because some people bought what water they could at the low, controlled price inside Charleston and then took it *outside* the price-controlled area to sell it at higher prices. Perversely, the price controls gave people an incentive to move water *away* from where it was needed most!

Prices provide information and incentives to both consumers and suppliers. What would a price of $10 a gallon have communicated to suppliers, including potential suppliers who would not ordinarily be in the bottled water business? To alert, enterprising people in surrounding states who had the ability to truck water to Charleston, the price would have said, "Bottled water is much more valuable in Charleston than here. Take a truckload to Charleston!"

We can imagine college students in Virginia and Georgia hearing of $10-per-gallon water in Charleston, renting a truck, buying all the water they could load into it from their local Walmarts, and driving all night with precious supplies of clean water. As soon as they open up their truck and start selling, they begin to relieve the scarcity, and prices start heading back down. Indeed, they might find that as the day goes on, and others with the same idea appear, they must offer their water for $9 a gallon, then $6, then $4, and so on. The high price of $10 a gallon creates the incentive for actions that bid it down.

By contrast, what did the enforced prehurricane price communicate? It said that the relative desire for and availability of bottled water in Charleston had not changed. That message, we might say, was a lie. At the same time, it carried no incentive for people to go out of their way to take bottled water to Charleston.

Let's consider now the case of gasoline-powered generators, whose prices rose from hundreds to thousands of dollars before the price controls were imposed. Again, the free-market price—let's call it $5,000—would communicate that people's desire for power generation was urgent, and the availability of generators was low. The high price would signal potential suppliers of generators to bring them to Charleston and dissuade Charlestonians from buying generators. So who *would* buy at that price; who would get the precious generators?

The seemingly automatic response I usually receive from my students is that "the rich" would spend $5,000 for a generator, because they are rich, whereas "the poor" would have to do without. "The rich" would have the benefits of electricity, then, and "the poor" would not. Try to go beyond this first answer, because it's not a good one.

* * * * *

One way to approach the question is to consider what kinds of people in Charleston have the most to gain from a supply of electricity and would therefore bid the most for a portable generator. Is it homeowners? Probably not. What would a grocer pay for a generator if she had $2,000's worth of frozen food in her freezers and $3,000's worth of perishables in her refrigerated cases, all beginning to warm up? What would a gas station owner pay for a generator if he had $5,000's worth of much-needed gasoline in his underground tanks, inaccessible because he had no electricity to power his pumps? What would a banker pay for a generator when his customers needed cash from his ATM, which was also without electricity?

Suppose the grocer, the gas station owner, and the banker had been able to buy the generators, because a $5,000 price tag deterred any homeowner from buying a generator that was much more useful to the community at the grocery store, gas station, or ATM. Who would have had the benefit of the electricity generated? Certainly the owners of those businesses would have benefited, but all their customers would have benefited too. Because electricity was much more valuable keeping perishables cold, gasoline flowing, and cash available, a high price for generators was just what the people of Charleston needed to maintain coordination among them all, by giving everyone an incentive to get electricity to where it could do the most good.

What happened, in fact, when the price controls were imposed and generators could legally be sold for no more than the $300 that they sold for before the storm? If you had been a hardware store owner with a couple of generators, what would you have done with them?

* * * * *

What was the effect of preventing "price gouging" on portable generators? Here is an illustrative story from Professor Russ Sobel, who was there at the time:

> My neighbor was high school best friends, years ago, with the now owner of a local hardware store. The store had two generators. He didn't get the store open before the price controls took effect. So he was faced with them. He kept one for his family and sold the other at the controlled price to my neighbor (like 1/10th of the free market price). My neighbor's daughter (who was my age . . . the "girl next door" cutie) was blow-drying her hair on it, and my dad was going over to use his electric shaver. In

the meantime, the gas station, the grocery store, the bank (with an ATM), and Kmart were all without power.[6]

What a dreadful waste of precious resources!

The Essential Role of Free-Market Prices

Freely determined market prices are society's essential means of communicating the vastly dispersed and ever-changing "knowledge of the particular circumstances of time and place."[7] We should free all our markets from price controls of any kind because we need market prices to give us this essential information in order to coordinate our various activities. Prices tell us what to do, or how to do it, by telling us indirectly what others know and what they are doing. Prices communicate to all, in a manner usable by all, the dispersed knowledge of all. Without market prices, we would face chaos and poverty. With market prices, we cooperate, coordinate our infinitely varied purposes, and prosper.

When public policy makes prices more rigid, or distorts prices away from market-determined levels, that policy impedes the communication function of prices, reduces the coordination among different people that market prices make possible, and thereby reduces overall well-being.

Interventions that distort prices away from free-market levels block communication and hinder coordination. In each case, the intervention brings about the kind of waste (though perhaps harder to detect) that occurred when Russ Sobel's neighbor dried her hair and his father used his electric shaver with electricity that could have kept thousands of dollars' worth of food from spoiling.

Every price has an important story to tell. Every single one should be left free. Good government will protect all people's freedom to negotiate whatever prices they see fit for the purchase or sale of their property, in peaceful negotiation with others.

Though market prices are essential to human flourishing, they don't guide us all by themselves. If we are to cooperate as well as possible in a society based on division of labor and exchange, we must use prices to discover how best to create value for others. That is, we must use prices to pursue profit and avoid loss, because profits—in a free market—come from creating value for other people. To profit and loss, and to their all-important role in making the world a better place, we turn in the next chapter.

10

Profit, Loss, and Discovery

In a world of endless possibilities but limited resources with which to try out those possibilities; in a world where many people have business ideas, but it's not clear which of those ideas are good ones; in a world where no single person even knows how to make a pencil, much less predict what new products, processes, and technologies will best serve people's needs a year or five years from now—in such a world, we need some means of sorting out the good ideas from the bad, for discovering which products and processes actually do serve us better than others.

We need free markets because they give us such a means of discovery: profit and loss. It is an imperfect means, to be sure, but it's the best available to us. Hence, here is the second of three principles of spontaneous economic order that account for why we need free markets:

> *In free markets, profit and loss help entrepreneurs discover the most value-creating uses of scarce resources, by providing them feedback about how well they are serving others: profit rewards value creation; loss punishes value destruction.*

This chapter explains what profit and loss are and what information they communicate. It lays out the indispensable role they play in helping entrepreneurs discover how to create value for others. It distinguishes admirable profit from blameworthy profit, explains that profits are more important as guides to future action than as rewards for past action, and draws conclusions for public policy.

What Profit and Loss Are; What They Mean

Let's start with this question to frame the discussion: how much profit is too much? I'd like readers to answer for themselves before reading on. I'll come back to it soon.

Many people think that profits for one person must come at the expense of another. The roots of this belief may be in Marxism, based as it is on the now-discredited labor theory of value we talked about in Chapter 1. On this view, profit is ugly because it can result only from exploitation. It is the difference between the objective, labor-determined value of the capitalist's product and the wages he pays his laborers. Because the laborers who produced it are the sole source of the product's value, they should be paid the whole value they create, but they aren't. The capitalist exploits them to the amount of his profit.

Consider a simple example. Suppose you are the capitalist owner of a tractor factory. In a year, you buy $4 million's worth of inputs—steel, tires, glass, copper wire, and so on—that your workers assemble into tractors that you sell for $5 million. According to Marxist theory, your workers have created $1 million's worth of new value. You pay them, however, only $900,000. Your $100,000 profit was all created by the workers, but you did not pay them for it. Your profit means you exploited your workers. You live as a parasite, at others' expense. Shame on you . . . if the labor theory were correct.

But it is not correct.

Consider the implications of the subjective theory of value, which supplanted the labor theory in "the marginal revolution." Because the value of a good is subjective—because different people value things differently—exchange can be (and is, except when we make mistakes) value creating for both parties. As long as each person gives up what she values less for what she values more, exchange creates value for both.

Each person gets more (according to her values) only when the other person also gets more (according to his different values).

In the tractor factory example, the wage rates the company must pay emerge from competition among workers for jobs and competition among companies for workers' services. The workers value their wages more than the time and effort they give the tractor factory, and the tractor factory values the workers' time and effort more than the wages it pays. Both sides benefit from the exchange. Whether the factory makes profits or losses is irrelevant to this fact (except that if losses go on too long, the wages must cease altogether).

Voluntary exchange is positive-sum. Wealth is *created* through trade, as long as we judge people's wealth by their own subjective valuations. One man's gain, in free and voluntary exchange, means another man's gain. On this view, profit is a very positive thing. It results not from exploitation but from creating new value for other people.

Exactly what are profit and loss, and where do they come from?[8]

To begin with, we should always keep them together in our thinking, like the two sides of a coin. Think of the market process not as a profit system but as a profit-and-loss system. Think of businesspeople not as profit makers but as people who risk loss in the hope of earning profit, and who frequently just make losses. The future is always uncertain; no one is guaranteed a profit.

Here's the definition: profit or loss equals yield minus cost:

$$\begin{array}{r} \text{Yield} \\ \underline{-\text{Cost}} \\ \text{Profit or Loss} \end{array}$$

This is the broadest definition of profit or loss. In everyday terms, it is the difference between what we get out of an effort (its yield) and what we put into it (its cost). If that difference is positive, it's profit; if it is negative, it's loss.

Yield properly understood comprises not just the monetary yield. People care about innumerable things other than money, such as working conditions, hours, how satisfying and interesting the work is, and so on. To get a full picture of yield, then, we should pay attention to nonmonetary benefits also.

But nonmonetary benefits are hard to quantify, and most people do care a lot about the money they make, so for now let us restrict our thinking about yield to monetary yield. The money part of yield is total revenue. It is the money customers pay the enterprise for its product. Cost is total cost, everything they spend or otherwise give up (such as alternative uses of the owners' time) to produce that product.

$$\begin{array}{cc}
\text{Yield} & \text{Total revenue} \\
\underline{-\text{Cost}} & \underline{-\text{Total cost}} \\
\text{Profit or Loss} & \text{Profit or Loss}
\end{array}$$

(with an arrow → between the two columns)

Consider the elements of this difference one at a time. First, what determines an enterprise's monetary yield, its total revenue, in a free-market setting?

The size of the (monetary) yield is determined by the customers who buy the enterprise's products; customers' valuations of the good or service determine the monetary yield to the entrepreneur. Customers will pay for something only what it is worth to them (or less). What they'll pay for the entrepreneur's output approximates the value of that product to them. So the entrepreneur's total revenue reflects the amount of value she has provided her customers.

Note that the value of a product to the customers is almost always *more than* what they have to pay. At the going price, some people get what they consider a decent bargain; some get what they consider a great bargain.[9] Hence, total revenue is a conservative indicator of the value the business provides to customers.

Now what determines a business's cost? As we discussed in Chapter 2, all costs are properly understood as opportunity costs, the values of the best opportunities forgone when an action is taken. The cost of production, then, is the next best uses of all the resources used in production; it is the value of what does *not* get produced instead.

Profit or loss, then, is the difference between the value an entrepreneur produces for customers and the value of the resources she uses in doing so.

Total revenue		Value of the output to the customers
−Total cost	→	−Values of inputs in their next best uses
Profit or Loss		Profit or Loss

The arithmetic is simple, isn't it? But look at what a profoundly important fact about enterprise it reveals: entrepreneurs make profits by increasing the value available from resources, that is, by *creating* value. On the other side of the coin, when entrepreneurs make losses, they destroy value.

Let's illustrate with an example. Suppose Alice develops and produces a new line of women's sportswear. She incurs a variety of costs. Among other things, she must rent space, purchase cloth and thread, rent or purchase sewing and cutting machines, buy electricity, and hire people to help her. All of those productive resources could be used to produce other things whose value is reflected in the price she must pay for the resources. For each resource she uses, she must outbid other entrepreneurs who would like to use it for some other purpose. Her space could be used to house some other business; the cloth and thread could be used to produce sheets or upholstery; some of the sewing and cutting machines could be used to produce other kinds of clothing; the electricity could be used for myriad other purposes; and the skills and energy of the people she hires could also be used in all sorts of ways. Don't forget alternative uses of Alice's own talent and energy; the most valuable service she could provide some other employer is the cost of Alice's being in business for herself.

The cost of Alice's sportswear, then, is the value to consumers of the best other things that might have been produced with the resources Alice uses on sportswear instead.

Now suppose Alice's total cost in a year is $100,000, but her customers pay her $120,000 for her sportswear. She makes a $20,000 profit. How? By taking resources worth $100,000 in their next best uses and transforming them into sportswear worth . . . $120,000! Alice has *created* $20,000's worth of new value for other people. She has put those resources to a higher-valued use than their best (known) alternatives. Her actions are profoundly creative. Her $20,000 profit is a consequence of her creating at least $20,000's worth of new value for consumers.

On this view, how much profit is too much?

No amount, right? The more the better. There can't be too much profit if it's made in a free market.

Suppose Alice were to make far more profit than $20,000. Suppose she had taken $100,000's worth of resources and transformed them into sportswear worth, say, $500,000. (I don't know how she would do that; perhaps through design genius.) Would her now profit of $400,000 be "too much" in some meaningful sense? How could it be? Too much for whom? Her customers clearly love her clothing. Her profit would mean she has produced for them far greater value out of existing scarce resources than others expect to be able to produce. That creativity is a great thing, not a bad thing. It serves others.

Or suppose that Alice finds an otherwise useless magic wand that conjures the sportswear out of thin air, so that her cost (other than the cost of her time) is zero. Assuming her customers will pay Alice $120,000 for her products, but she uses no scarce resources of buildings, machines, electricity, labor, and so on in production, Alice's profit would be the entire $120,000 she gets paid (an infinite return on an investment of zero!). Would that be bad for others? Of course not. In that case, we would have sportswear we willingly pay $120,000 for without having to give up any other goods that we would have had to give up if Alice required scarce resources in order to produce.

The more profit, the better for society, as long as that profit is made in a free market.

Next, consider loss. Suppose Alice takes resources worth $100,000 in other uses and transforms them into sportswear for which people will pay only, say, $70,000. She thereby has a loss of $30,000. What does this loss mean? It means she has destroyed $30,000's worth of value to others. In place of a variety of other goods and services worth $100,000 to us consumers, we now have sportswear worth only $70,000. Our society is $30,000 worse off than we would have been if Alice had never tried her enterprise.

The huge losses that some companies make represent huge losses to society overall. Consider the dramatic true story of Iridium, a satellite phone company backed by Motorola that went bankrupt in 1999. The concept was wonderful: a person with an Iridium phone could call from anywhere in the world to anywhere in the world. The phone would beam a signal up from anywhere in the world to one of 66 satellites in low-Earth orbit. Computers in the satellites would beam the signal to the satellite closest over the person being called and down to his Iridium phone, or to a receiving tower located near him, with the call completed over landlines. It was like a worldwide cell phone system, but with only 66 "cell phone towers" in the sky.

The money cost of the Iridium system was an estimated $5 billion to $7 billion. The company developed communications satellites, launched 66 of them, designed and debugged the software to run the system, built ground towers, negotiated with governments around the world for permission to build those towers and run landlines, and so on. It was a tremendous undertaking. All the resources Iridium used—the time and energy of the satellite designers and manufacturers, the rocketry, the time and expertise of the software designers, the computers, the construction of the ground towers, the time and expertise of the negotiators—all those resources could have been used to produce other things that you and I would have valued. Instead, they were used to produce the Iridium system.

In the end, the system could attract only a few thousand customers, instead of the millions it needed to turn a profit. The phones were very expensive, they were large and heavy ("like bricks"), and they performed poorly indoors. More important, the people at Iridium grossly underestimated the rates of growth and improvement of their main competitor—cell phones. Iridium simply could not compete with them. Around the time of bankruptcy in 2000, they were even preparing to deorbit the satellites, letting them fall into the atmosphere and burn up, rather than clutter the space around Earth with useless junk.[10]

Iridium was a stunning technical accomplishment but a staggering economic failure. Its losses were in the billions.

Why? Because it destroyed value. The company took resources valued at between $5 billion and $7 billion in other uses and transformed them into satellite phone services valued at almost nothing. It was a minor tragedy.

Profit, then, is a consequence of the entrepreneur's creating new value; loss is the consequence of the entrepreneur's destroying value. Larger profits mean more new value created. In the same way that prices reflect information about how badly people need things and how easy (or hard) it is to produce those things, profit and loss tell how much value people have created or destroyed. Accordingly, there is simply no such thing as too much profit, as long as that profit is made in voluntary, free-market exchange. The more profit, the better.

The Crucial Social Role of Profit and Loss: Discovery

Because productive resources such as human talent, machinery, energy, and raw materials are scarce, whenever we use resources to produce one thing, we thereby give up all the other things we could have used those resources to produce instead. To live as prosperously as possible, therefore, we need to put resources to their most valuable uses.

But just what the most valuable uses are at any time and place is uncertain because of the limitations on what any one individual can know (remember that no one even knows how to make a pencil) and because the future is inherently uncertain. Profit and loss help us discover what to do to get the greatest possible value out of our scarce resources.

Discovery of the Best (Known) Uses of (Known) Resources

Recall the thought experiment from Chapter 8 about getting a railroad line from one city to another when a mountain range lies between them. To build it in the least costly way to society overall, should it be built through the mountains, using more engineering and less steel, or around the mountains, using more steel and less engineering? For society overall, the best way to go is whichever is cheapest—whichever way yields the greatest profit.

Such calculations of expected profit or loss, based on expected market prices, are indispensable for helping entrepreneurs discover how best to use scarce resources to satisfy the wants of others.

Of course, entrepreneurs' forward-looking estimates of profit and loss are not their only means of discovering the most value-creating uses of scarce resources in an uncertain world. That discovery also occurs through backward-looking calculations of the actual profits or losses they have made on their different projects. In reading that bottom line, they discover whether they have used scarce resources well or badly, whether they have created or destroyed value. Then (if they have enough cash flow to continue in business at all) it's back to their entrepreneurial judgments: What does the profit or loss mean? Why was it different from what was expected? How might losses be cut or profits increased?

Realized profit or loss never tells an entrepreneur what to do next; it only makes clear the past project's success or failure in creating value for others. But that feedback is essential in guiding entrepreneurs as they judge what to do next.

Discovery of the New and Better: "Creative Destruction"

In addition to this discovery of how best to use known means to achieve known ends, profit and loss direct the discovery of *previously unknown* ways to satisfy human wants: new products; new resources; new productive techniques, tools, and processes. This is innovation, discovery of real novelty that helps us make more out of life. For innovation also, profit and loss are indispensable.

Economist Joseph Schumpeter called this kind of discovery "creative destruction." He meant the destruction of goods, processes, and enterprises that once served people well by the creation of new goods, new processes, and new enterprises that serve us better.[11]

For example, consider how we light our buildings. The primary means used to be whale-oil lamps. Then we discovered that petroleum could be refined into kerosene, a cheaper fuel that burned brighter and cleaner. The creation of kerosene destroyed whale oil's role in lighting and with it large portions of the whaling industry.

Kerosene's role in lighting was creatively destroyed in its turn by the development of electric lighting—cheaper, brighter, and cleaner. What will creatively destroy electric light bulbs and fluorescent tubes? As of this writing, it looks as if it might be LEDs (light-emitting diodes), but of course it's impossible to tell. Human ingenuity might come up with something else entirely!

Consider telecommunications. Fifty years ago, when someone in the United States called someone in Australia, the signal of her voice was carried by copper wire—tons and tons of copper torn from the mountains of Peru and Utah and Montana—stretching in a cable across the Pacific Ocean. The call could be made, but quality was poor, and there were delays and clicks as repeaters amplified the steadily degrading signal.

Now when we make a phone call to Australia, the signal of our voice is carried either by an optical fiber cable or by microwave. Optical fiber cables are also stretched across the Pacific, but they carry thousands of times as many calls as copper for their weight, and they are made from cheap and abundant sand. Microwave communication requires even less physical stuff: we just bounce the signal off a satellite. The calls are cheap, there are no delays, and the quality is almost perfect. Telecommunication via optical fibers and microwaves is creatively destroying communication via copper cable.

Innovation, then—beyond the discovery of how best to use known resources for known ends—is discovery of new and better resources, or new ways to use them, or formerly unknown ends. Profit and loss continuously motivate and guide innovation.

Why Profit and Loss Are Necessary to Human Advancement

In this role of guiding innovation, profit and loss are not just helpful; they are indispensable. The reason has to do with scarcity and uncertainty.

Resources for experimentation are scarce. Lots of people have ideas for new products and processes, but most of those ideas probably won't work, and we don't have enough capital to invest in them all. Machinery, energy, and human talent invested in one idea are unavailable to be invested in another idea, so only some ideas can be tried out.

At the same time, just what are the best new ideas—"best" in how they satisfy others' wants—cannot be known ahead

PROFIT, LOSS, AND DISCOVERY

of time. Businesspeople can never be certain that their ideas will work. They must try to figure out, to imagine, to project what will work well enough and at low enough cost so that the price it earns will cover that cost.

Human beings simply don't know for sure what products and processes will fit well into the ever-unfolding future. The following quotations should help make this clear:

> This "telephone" has too many shortcomings to be seriously considered as a means of communication. The device is inherently of no value to us.
> —William Orton, president of Western Union, America's largest telecommunications company, in 1876

> The wireless music box has no imaginable commercial value. Who would pay for a message sent to nobody in particular?
> —One of David Sarnoff's associates in response to his urgings for investment in radio in the 1920s

> Who the hell wants to hear actors talk? The music— that's the big plus about this.
> —H. M. Warner, president of Warner Brothers, on adding sound to movies in 1927

We don't like their sound, and guitar music is on the way out.

—Decca Records on rejecting the Beatles in 1962

So we went to Atari and said, "Hey, we've got this amazing thing, even built with some of your parts, and what do you think about funding us? Or we'll give it to you. We just want to do it. Pay our salary, we'll come work for you." And they said, "No." So then we went to Hewlett-Packard, and they said, "Hey, we don't need you. You haven't got through college yet."

—Apple Computer Inc. founder Steve Jobs on attempts to get Atari and HP interested in his and Steve Wozniak's personal computer

Those remarkable quotations show that even people in the best position to predict what sorts of products and processes will be worth trying often get it wrong. Who was better able to assess the prospects of a satellite phone system than the people at Motorola? Yet they misjudged. More than one major publishing house rejected J.K. Rowling's idea for the *Harry Potter* series. Think what a dreadful misjudgment *that* was. In general, it's very difficult to judge what enterprises really will create value for others; over half of all new businesses fail within the first five years. We human beings are woefully ignorant about what to do today to improve our standard of living tomorrow. We have to experiment.

Profit and loss guide the experimentation.

Entrepreneurs with exciting new ideas peer into an uncertain future and judge the likelihood of developments in consumer tastes, production technologies, labor costs, shipping costs, and all the other considerations they expect to affect the success or failure of the project(s) they are considering. On the basis of past and present prices, they estimate future prices of everything relevant and calculate the project's likely profit or loss. These forward-looking profit-and-loss calculations guide entrepreneurs to discover which possible endeavors promise to create the most new value for customers.

Once entrepreneurs have committed themselves and tied up scarce resources in producing various goods and services, the consuming public needs some means of sorting out the good ideas from the bad. We need a feedback system that tells entrepreneurs when they actually are creating value and when they are destroying it, and that motivates them to do more of the former and less of the latter. Actual, realized profits and losses do that job. When a new product or process—like Iridium—shows itself unlikely to serve society well by piling up losses, its backers are "told" by those losses to stop wasting resources on it. On the other hand, when a new product or process serves the public well, profits reward its backers and encourage them to develop it further.

Profit and loss are society's indispensable guidance system for economic activity.

Market-Based Profit versus Legal Plunder

This chapter so far has sung the praises of the profit-and-loss system: trade creates wealth; profit results from creating new value; the more profit the better for society. In each case, I have added a crucial proviso: *as long as that profit is made in a free market.* The underlying discipline of the free market's basic institutions—private property and freedom of exchange—will direct profit-seeking activities in socially useful, mutually beneficial directions.

When government intervenes, however, profit may come from seizing wealth rather than creating it. Where governments transfer property from those who own it to those who don't, or restrict the freedom to engage in mutually beneficial exchange, or fail to enforce contracts; or where government ownership allows someone to pollute or deplete what "everybody owns," then profit can be made at the expense of others. Such profit making merits not praise but blame.

The crucial factor for distinguishing the good kind of profit from the bad is mutual consent of the parties involved. Such interactions occur by what German sociologist Franz Oppenheimer calls the "economic means"—free and voluntary exchange.[12] In contrast to the economic means are what Oppenheimer calls the "political means" of transferring goods without the consent of those concerned: taxing, restricting, granting monopolies, licensing, subsidizing, and the like. When political means are used, it is not necessary to get the consent of those one deals with. Those possessing government power simply compel others, often harming them thereby.

We should endorse and celebrate profits that are earned in free markets, because they come from creating value for other people. We should condemn profits made through the political means, because they come from transferring rather than creating value and they provide misleading signals about where human effort and other resources should be applied to help humanity flourish.

Guidance for the Future; Not Reward for the Past

Before we close this discussion of profit and loss, I want to acknowledge the concern that sometimes profits (or losses) earned in a free market are simply unfair, and therefore that such profits or losses or the actions that lead to them should be restricted.

To return to the last chapter's discussion of price gouging, for example, consider the high profits made by merchants who sell bottled water or generators after a hurricane for 5 or 10 times the normal price. Those profits don't seem fair. The store owners have done nothing brilliant to merit those high profits; they just got lucky. And they got lucky because others got unlucky. Why should the economic system reward them?

Some ask the same thing about the large profits made in recent years by oil companies. If prices go up just because of increasing demand from India and China, and through no foresight or hard work of the oil companies themselves, why should the economic system reward them?

On the loss side, we might claim that it is unfair for firms to be driven to bankruptcy by economic forces beyond their control. Why should the economic system punish them? These firms or industries are said to deserve a bailout at taxpayer expense.

I leave to other writers and other books the (to me compelling) philosophical and ethical reasons for not interfering with free-market profit and loss and focus instead on the practical, economic reason. That is, what society requires from profit and loss is not *reward* for past action but *guidance* for future action.

Forward-looking profit-and-loss projections together with backward-looking profit-and-loss accounting give entrepreneurs indispensable (though not infallible) guidance for what to do today to make the world a better place tomorrow. And we can't have that future guidance without rewarding past results—even those that result from dumb luck. Profit and loss do reward or punish *past* actions, true, but that is not their essential function in society, not the crucial job they do for us. It's just the means of carrying out that function, of doing that job. Their essential function is to guide *future* action by entrepreneurs.

As we have seen, the high prices of bottled water and generators right after a hurricane—and the high profits they promise—tell anyone watching to bring bottled water and generators to the stricken area. The high price of gasoline early in the current decade—and the high profits it caused— told oil companies to expand exploration and production. They did, and those efforts made possible the increased output that has brought gasoline prices back down now in 2015 as I write. The losses suffered in the financial crisis by thousands of investors in mortgage-backed securities who credulously relied on the securities' AAA credit ratings tell everyone watching to investigate risk more carefully before investing, lest they lose their capital. (Of course, that lesson is weakened to the extent that investors are bailed out with taxpayers' money.)

The main job of free-market profits and losses is not to do moral justice for past action but to give practical guidance for future action. Their crucial role is future oriented. Reward or punishment for past actions is the incidental means, not the essential end. Looking backward at profits or losses realized from past projects, entrepreneurs see how well they created value for others. On the basis of that information, their own judgment, and current and expected prices, they make profit-or-loss estimates for various other projects they might undertake in the future. When they choose the ones they expect to be most profitable, in the expectation that they will enjoy the profit or suffer the loss, society benefits.

Summary and Implications for Policy

The implications of this insight for public policy are straightforward: We should free our markets of all interference with profit-and-loss feedback. Policies that leave entrepreneurs free to innovate and get straight profit-and-loss feedback from the public will foster rapid discovery of new and better ways to satisfy the public's wants. Policies that restrict entrepreneurs' freedom—that limit the profits of those who serve the public well or shield from losses those who serve the public poorly—will slow down rates of increase in overall well-being.

Society has no better gauge of the contribution an enterprise makes to the world than its profit or loss in an unhampered market. Its profitability is a kind of summary judgment that comprises the individual judgments of everyone concerned. In judging which enterprises should be tried out, which should expand, and which should close down, we have no better tool than entrepreneurial innovation and profit-and-loss selection in a free market.

* * * * *

Though this chapter has emphasized the informational role of profit and loss in telling businesspeople what to do and how, profit and loss play a motivational role also. In a free market, where interactions are voluntary on both sides, people can profit only when they create benefits for others. Hence, in free markets, everyone has a strong incentive to serve others. In government interventions, by contrast, where legal force is used to compel or forbid some interaction even against another's will, incentives to serve others are weak or absent. And incentives matter. This brings us to the third main reason that we need free markets, the subject of our next chapter.

11

Institutions and Incentives

The foundational institutions of a free market are private ownership and freedom of exchange. After all, what is a market but a legal setting in which the private owners of goods and services voluntarily exchange them with others?

It turns out that these foundational institutions not only make possible the market prices and the profit-and-loss signals that tell us *how* to create value for others, they also give us the incentive to do so. When we are required to respect the property rights of others, and when we are free to exchange with others—or not—as we choose, market forces arise that help us overcome the inclination to be selfishly inconsiderate of the desires of others and to cultivate in its place a respectful attention to those desires. Private ownership and freedom of exchange restrain and even penalize our baser instincts and require us to benefit others if we are to benefit ourselves.

Even well-intended uses of government power, by contrast, allow people to get what they want from others without getting their agreement.

We can state this as the third of three principles of spontaneous economic order that account for why human beings need free markets:

> *Private ownership and freedom of exchange, the foundational institutions of a free market, lead people to serve others in order to benefit themselves; whereas government interventions tempt people to benefit themselves at others' expense.*

In the first part of this chapter, we'll contrast the incentives inherent in private ownership and government ownership. In the second part, we'll contrast the incentives in free exchange and government interference with voluntary exchange—government "regulation."

Let's approach the different incentives in private and government ownership with a real-world example of each.

The Incentives of Ownership

The Tongass National Forest blankets the Pacific coast in southeastern Alaska. The nation's largest national forest, larger than West Virginia, it is also the largest temperate-zone rainforest in the world. It is a magnificent land of densely wooded islands, bays, and inlets. It is home to grizzly bears, wolverines, Sitka black-tailed deer, bald eagles, and 800-year-old Sitka spruce rising 250 feet into the sky. Some 30 percent of all Pacific salmon spawn in its streams.

Major industrial logging operations have occurred in the Tongass for about the past four decades. The U.S. Forest Service, responsible for managing the forest as a "Land of Many Uses," builds logging roads into the forest and leases the right to take timber to private companies. The logging companies then sell the timber on the open market.

The logging causes environmental damage. Much of the forest's old-growth timber has been cut down. Thousands of miles of heavy logging roads crisscross the forest. Erosion from the logging operations has silted up the streams. The siltation makes it harder for salmon to spawn. That is a serious economic problem for the region because its main industry is fishing.

As painful as this damage to the Tongass is to most of us, we might justify it if the value of the timber taken out of the

Tongass were sufficiently high. But, remarkably, the market value of the timber taken out is less than the value of the resources used up in getting it out. In the words of economist John Baden:

> The economic costs of securing the timber far exceeded any commercial value the timber had. . . . Roads funded at taxpayer expense allowed access to timber that was too sparse, too marginal, or too slow-growing to justify the high price of the roads and other development costs. In essence, taxpayers are subsidizing environmentally destructive behavior that no private timber company or private landowner would ever consider.[13]

As of 2004, the latest year for which the U.S. Forest Service's website provided information, the logging companies paid an average of $42.54 per 1,000 board feet of timber they extracted. But the Forest Service spent on average "between $300 and $400" per 1,000 board feet. By those estimates, the program lost between 85 cents and 89 cents out of every dollar. The website attributes the dramatic difference to the "low value of western hemlock lumber," the cost—"as high as $500,000/mile pending stream crossing needs and a host of other high cost items"—of logging roads "that will support a loaded truck over muskeg or floating bog soils," and generally "difficult access since the land consists of forested islands."[14]

Fortunately, the logging operations in the Tongass have been scaled way back in recent years. But the question remains: why would the Forest Service sponsor this environmentally damaging, economically senseless logging in the Tongass for decades?

To help you think through this question, here is a useful technique for policy analysis that distills some of the wisdom of *public choice economics*, the branch of economics that studies the choices made by people in the public sector:

Of any policy, ask two questions:

1. What groups are primarily affected?

2. What are their incentives?

Those incentives will determine (or strongly influence) the outcomes.

How would you answer those questions for the Tongass? Think it over before continuing.

* * * * *

The groups with the most obvious financial interest in the logging program are, of course, the logging interests—the logging companies, loggers, and local sawmills. The logging companies lease the right to take timber from the Tongass, and because they don't pay for the logging roads as they would if they owned the land, a large portion of their costs is borne by taxpayers. The loggers and sawyers benefit from high-paying jobs, and the owners of the logging companies benefit from profits that would not exist in the absence of the taxpayer-financed roads.

Follow the money. Who funds the thousands of miles of roads the logging companies use? The funding comes from another group with a major interest in the Tongass logging program—the U.S. Forest Service, which administers the program. What is the Forest Service's interest? Well, the program is huge, and a source of substantial revenue to the U.S. Forest Service (even as it is a large drain on the U.S. Treasury). In fact, as early as 1985, "about 342,000 miles of roads [had] been constructed under the auspices of the Forest Service . . . , more than eight times the total mileage of the U.S. Interstate Highway System."[15] The program means a huge budget, many offices, many studies to do, and many Forest Service jobs.

Follow the money back another step to find another group with an interest in the program: Who provides the Forest Service's funding? Congress does. What benefit does Congress realize from logging the Tongass at a loss? Who might support Congress for supporting this program? The logging companies and those in related industries do. Alaska's senators and representative receive substantial campaign contributions and other political support from the logging interests to encourage them to keep the logging subsidies coming to Alaska. The legislators have a strong incentive to vote for the logging program to please their constituents and keep those campaign contributions coming.

(Of course, Alaska has only a few members of Congress, but they and the politicians from other timber states gain majority support for the logging program by promising to vote for the pet programs of their colleagues in nontimber states in return.)

These are the incentives that sustained the logging, year after year. The loggers supported their members of Congress, the members of Congress supported the Forest Service, and the Forest Service supported the loggers. Each group had strong financial and career incentives to keep this program going.

Of course, one other important group is hidden in this picture—the taxpayer-citizens. Our role is to surrender to the Internal Revenue Service the money that finances the whole works. Because the loss-making logging in the Tongass is so much *against* our interests, both financial and environmental, we may ask, "Why don't we stop it?"

The answer public choice economics gives is that most taxpayers don't know about it, as they don't know about most of the programs that take money out of their pockets and put it into the pockets of special-interest groups. It makes no sense for them to know because the cost (to them as individuals) of doing something about it is far greater than the cost (to them as individuals) of the program itself. The costs of the program are spread over all taxpayers, so the per-person tax cost is small, maybe a few dollars. It would be far more costly in time and effort for any taxpayer to actively oppose the program. Merely parking in Washington for a day while one went to complain to one's representatives would cost a lot more than one individual's share of the tax. And the likelihood of making a difference is very low. Accordingly, taxpayers have a very weak incentive to try to stop the logging program and other legislation that benefits special-interest groups at the expense of the general public.

Now for a question crucial to understanding the perverse incentives driving the spoliation:

Who owns the Tongass?

That question has three different but equivalent answers. The first is "Everybody owns it." That is true in a sense: we all have some right to the national forests and the privilege to use them according to guidelines set out by the Forest Service.

The second answer at first sounds very different: "Nobody owns it." This too is true in a sense: no identifiable person or group has an exclusive right to use, control, and dispose of the national forests as they see fit.

The third answer is, "The government owns it." Ultimately, these seemingly different answers turn out to be different versions of the same one. What everyone owns, no one owns. That everyone owns something means that no one person or group has the privileges of ownership—the right to the use, control, and disposal. You are an "owner" of the Tongass, but can you sell your share? Do you have any say in the decisions about how it is used? No. The Tongass is best understood as government owned, because the government determines its use, control, and disposal.

That, I will suggest, is the problem. But first, let's consider a counterexample.

The Paul J. Rainey Wildlife Sanctuary is a 26,800-acre marshland owned by the Audubon Society. According to John Baden, the sanctuary "is a home for deer, armadillo, muskrat, otter, [and] mink," and 100,000 migrating snow geese use it to rest and feed. Baden tells an interesting story about Rainey, however, that helps us understand the incentives of private ownership. He writes that "since the early 1950s, thirty-seven wells have pumped natural gas (and a small amount of oil) at various times" from the sanctuary.[16]

That's a surprise. Most of us would expect a conservation group such as the Audubon Society to reject with horror the approaches of an oil company—an *oil* company!—that wanted to put drilling rigs, with their inevitable noise and unsightliness, not to mention possible pollution problems, into a *bird sanctuary*. And yet, until 1999 when leases expired, oil and gas were extracted from the Rainey Sanctuary. What do you think happened such that oil companies were admitted there? It wasn't government intervention; the Audubon Society's property rights were respected. So what happened?

Again, ask two questions:

1. What groups are primarily affected?

2. What are their incentives?

Those incentives will determine (or strongly influence) the outcomes.

* * * * *

One group primarily affected was the oil companies. They had a strong incentive to *make oil production in the wildlife preserve advantageous to conservationists*. The other primarily affected group was the Audubon Society, of course, which has a strong incentive to protect the wildlife in the Rainey Sanctuary but also to protect other wildlife elsewhere too. The oil companies offered the Audubon Society a deal. They would let the conservationists set the terms on which they would allow oil production in Rainey, including very substantial royalties. Baden reports that the "managers of Rainey found that the timing, placement, operation and structure of oil exploration could be carefully planned in conjunction with the seasonal requirements of wildlife, and adverse environmental effects could be avoided." The oil companies offered to route their roads over the least sensitive lands. Company operators had the ability to drill at an angle, so they could site their drills on unimportant land and still reach the expected oil and gas deposits. They agreed to suspend operations in nesting season. And they agreed to pay Audubon well. Over the years, Audubon earned over $25 million in royalties from its gas and oil. With that revenue, it maintained Rainey and also bought additional land on which to preserve still more wildlife.

As of January 2010, the officers of Rainey were investigating further leases in hopes of earning more revenue with which to maintain and improve the sanctuary.

Rainey gives us a marvelous example of dual use of a resource. From that beautiful marshland, society gains both wildlife preservation *and* more abundant natural gas. The oil company benefits. Audubon benefits. Homeowners who heat their houses with natural gas benefit. There are benefits all the way around.

Contrast the management of the Tongass National Forest and the Rainey Wildlife Sanctuary. In the former, we have serious environmental degradation at a substantial financial loss. In the latter, we have both environmental and energy benefits. In the one, the physical resource is allowed to deteriorate; in the other, it is carefully maintained.

What explains the difference? Is Tongass run by bad people and Rainey by good? No. The difference is in the different forms of ownership and their corresponding incentives. Tongass is owned by everybody, therefore by nobody. Decisions about it are made by government bureaucrats with no ownership stake in the land. When the logging operation loses money, there is no particular owner who feels and notices that loss. Accordingly, no one has a compelling incentive to stop the damage and red ink.

Why is Rainey so different? Because it is privately owned. As owner, the Audubon Society has a strong incentive to make the best possible use of the resource to achieve the organization's goals. The resource is a precious asset, *all* aspects of which must be tapped in order for Audubon to benefit as much as possible.

In recent decades, a number of environmental economists—sometimes known as "free-market environmentalists"—have studied the consequences of private and government ownership on the stewardship of natural resources. The essence of their "new resource economics" is as follows: Because private owners enjoy any profits and suffer any losses flowing from a resource, they have a strong incentive to use it in ways that satisfy the actual wants and needs of others at reasonable cost. Others communicate their wants and needs by the prices they offer. The owners notice the profit opportunities that these prices present for different uses of their resources. They choose the most highly valued combination of uses because they bear the opportunity cost of the choices they make. Had Audubon Society, for example, yielded to pressure from radical environmentalists and shut down gas production in Rainey, it would have borne the opportunity cost of that decision—the royalties it could earn and the improvements to the sanctuary those royalties could finance.

With government ownership of resources, the incentives are entirely different. The public servants charged with managing those resources, well-intentioned though they may be, do not have an ownership stake. They get paid a salary. If the resource is used profitably, they receive no bonus; if it is used at a loss or damaged, they suffer no personal loss or reduction in pay. Because they do not stand to profit from discovering any new and *better* uses of the resources than those the legislature dictates, they are not alert to such possibilities.

In other words, those public servants do not bear the opportunity cost of use. In the Tongass, the Forest Service does not experience the operating losses; taxpayers do. The Forest Service would not realize any savings that would accrue from stopping the waste.

Accordingly, the public administrators in charge of government-owned resources have a much weaker incentive to use them so as to serve the public well. They have a strong incentive, however, to serve the interests that support them politically and to protect their turf. The Forest Service serves the logging interests and their congressional overseers in order to keep the subsidy dollars flowing, regardless of what happens to the Tongass.

The contrast between the Tongass and Rainey shows the importance of the institution of private ownership for giving people an incentive to use their property to serve others in order to benefit themselves.

A similar point can be made about the institution of free exchange.

The Incentives in Freedom of Exchange and Restriction of Exchange

Should competent adults be allowed to exchange freely with one another? That is, should we be legally permitted to exchange our property and services with one another on mutually agreeable terms?

Most of us would answer yes to the question when it's asked this way. In principle, we believe in freedom of exchange—people should be allowed to do as they see fit with their own as long as they don't harm anyone else, and they should be allowed to decide the terms on which they interact with others. Of course.

But though most of us support freedom of exchange in principle, many reject it in practice: they support particular restrictions on exchange. They support occupational licensing to protect people from incompetent practitioners, zoning restrictions to foster better-planned communities, minimum-wage laws to raise incomes, antitrust regulation to prevent monopolies, Food and Drug Administration restrictions on the sale of pharmaceuticals to ensure their safety and effectiveness, and so on. All of these practices restrict freedom of exchange. They prevent competent adults from exchanging their property and services on mutually agreeable terms.

When people hedge their commitment to freedom of exchange and support some restriction of it, they usually do so because they believe the restriction will make people better off. They believe unrestricted freedom of exchange would harm people.

This section argues that this belief has it exactly backward. In practice, restrictions on freedom, *even when well intended*, almost always make people worse off. Why? Because when government force may be used, those who are able to control that force have little incentive to consider the well-being of others and to get the consent of others. They can just use that force to their own advantage at others' expense.

Conversely, unrestricted freedom of exchange—so long as it's peaceful and not fraudulent—gives people a strong incentive to consider others' wants, as doing so is the only way to get what *they* want. Freedom of exchange—and freedom to refuse unwanted exchanges—thereby unleashes powerful market forces that regulate very effectively in the public interest.

Let's illustrate the dangers of allowing governments to restrict freedom of exchange with a story about hairdressing.

Example: Hairdresser Licensing
In every U.S. state, in order to cut or dress somebody's hair for pay, a person must first obtain a cosmetology license from

that state. Generally, one must go to beauty school or serve an apprenticeship and then take a qualifying test. Once one has the license, one may practice; without it, one may not.

The avowed purpose of hairdresser regulation is "to protect the public health and safety."

Hairdresser licensing interferes with freedom of exchange. It is not enforced by invitation and polite request. Like all regulations, it is enforced by the police. If someone is caught dressing hair without a license, the practitioner can be fined and her practice shut down, even if the hairdresser and her customers both desire the transaction. They are not free, under the law, to exchange money and hairdressing services as they see fit.

Now, apply our quick public choice analysis to hairdresser licensing. What groups are most affected by licensing? And what are their incentives? Hairdressers themselves are the group most affected, of course. Let's illuminate their incentives with a story.

In the mid-1980s, I was speaking to an eighth-grade history class in Baltimore, describing some of the problems with occupational licensing that Walter Williams describes in *The State Against Blacks*. I was explaining Williams's claim that hairdresser licensing is often stacked against low-income people when a thoughtful-looking black student in the third row raised her hand and said, "That happened to me."

Her name was Sharissa. She told us that one of the five-year-olds in her neighborhood was having a birthday party, and the girls going to the party wanted their hair done in gold braid. That involves braiding the hair close to the scalp, weaving gold thread through the braids in decorative patterns, and then curling the bangs in front. Sharissa was good at it, and because she wanted to buy a new outfit, she dressed some of the little girls' hair for $5 each. In all, she braided the hair of about 10 children, some at her house and some at the children's houses. She estimated her income at about $50 and her expenses, for gold twine and styling gel, at about $6.75. She netted enough to buy her new outfit.

But that's not the end of the story.

A neighbor stopped Devin, one of Sharissa's young clients, on the sidewalk one day and asked, "Who did your hair for you?"

"'Rissy did it," said Devin. That night, Sharissa's mother received a call from a neighbor. The neighbor said she had heard that Sharissa was doing hair without a license. That was illegal, and she should stop. Sharissa's mother reluctantly told Sharissa to cancel her other appointments. "We don't want any trouble."

Sharissa found out later that the woman who had stopped the child and asked, "Who did your hair for you?" has a niece . . . a licensed hairdresser, who had had a $32 appointment canceled by the mother of one of Sharissa's five-year-old clients.

On the basis of this story, what would you say is the actual purpose of hairdresser regulation, as opposed to its official purpose, if in fact there is a difference?

In trying to understand the effects of government regulations that interfere with free exchange, concentrate on the incentives those regulations generate. Ask yourself, where hairdressers must get a license from the state in order to practice, what are the incentives for licensed hairdressers with respect to licensing? Do they want more or less restrictive licensing?

As the case of Sharissa and her little neighbors shows, the actual effect of licensing is to hinder competition. It blocked Sharissa from earning some income, it forced the five-year-olds' parents to pay sixfold higher prices, and it protected the income of the licensed hairdresser. This effect in Sharissa's neighborhood generalizes to all licensing everywhere. Licensing blocks competition and thereby supports the incomes of the already-licensed practitioners. Accordingly— and this is crucial—the existence of licensing gives licensed practitioners a strong incentive to support licensing requirements that are strict and strictly enforced, regardless of their effect on the public health and safety.

The actual purpose of hairdresser licensing is to block competition in order to raise the prices that licensed hairdressers can charge. This fact is clear from the details of the licensing regulations, which include a few obvious requirements pertaining to health and safety but mostly restrict who is allowed to practice. In relation to supply and demand, these restrictions reduce the supply of legal hairdressing, shifting the curve up and left, consequently raising the prices we must pay for it.

Hairdresser licensing illustrates what economists call the "capture of regulation." The basic idea is as follows: Whenever governments regulate a particular industry, the dominant enterprises within that industry are strongly affected by the regulations. Accordingly, they have a strong incentive to influence those regulations in their own favor. They strive to influence the regulators and regulations, acting through their industry associations and lobbyists. Eventually, they come to direct the regulatory process more or less. The influence of the regulated group results in part from the necessities of regulation: Who knows enough about an industry to craft appropriate regulations? The members of that industry do, of course. For that reason, industry representatives are almost inevitably in a position to influence the regulations, if not to write them directly.

When representatives of the dominant groups in an industry control the regulatory process, we say that the regulation has been "captured" by the regulated group. They direct the regulation not in the public interest but in their own particular interest, often at the expense of their politically weaker competitors and the general public.

The point of this story of regulatory capture is a more general one. Humans are resourceful beings. When regulatory authority offers us the possibility of getting what we want by force rather than by creating value, many of us fall prey to the temptation.

Government intervention in any area of human relationships carries a serious risk of coming under the control of a special-interest group because it introduces force into those relationships. Intervention makes it possible for special-interest groups to get what they want from others without the others' consent. The sheer availability of legal force creates a nearly irresistible incentive for people to use that force to personal advantage. They organize, they lobby, they manipulate the governmental force for personal gain, disregarding harm to others.

Economics has a term for this kind of effort to influence government intervention in the economy for one's special benefit: "rent seeking." "Rent," in this sense of the word, is income derived from possession of a special privilege. The effort of merely seeking those privileges, instead of producing valuable goods or services, is wasteful. Worse is the economic distortion caused by the privileges themselves.

Regulation by Market Forces

This is not to say that there should be no regulation of the quality and safety of goods and services. Not at all. Rather, it is to say that regulation by market forces works better than government regulation, and the freer a market is from governmental restrictions, the stronger will be the competitive forces that regulate it.

To regulate is to make regular and orderly, to hold to a standard, to control according to rule, as a thermostat regulates the temperature in a building. Market forces regulate continuously, as competing businesses offer what they hope will be good value, customers choose among the various offerings, competing businesses react to those customer choices, and then customers choose again. That process is the market's regulator. Whereas government regulation works by the restriction of choice, restriction that is often captured by special interests, regulation by market forces relies on the exercise of choice.

Suppose there were no hairdresser licensing. Suppose state legislatures repealed or "sunsetted" their hairdresser licensing laws, relying thereafter only on freedom of exchange and regulation by market forces—what would happen? In a true free market for hairdressing, what forces would pressure hairdressers toward safety and quality?

How do people choose their hairdressers now, in the presence of licensing? How many base their choices on their hairdressers' license? Probably very few. Most of us rely primarily on experience. We try a hairdresser or barber, and if we like the results, we go back. If not, we go elsewhere. Hairdressers' need for repeat business, along with customers' freedom to go elsewhere, is enough by itself to enforce pretty high standards of quality.

Thus, the most important regulator in the market is competition itself, which subjects every business to the continuous judgment of the consuming public, who are free at every moment to give their business to a competitor.

Note that meaningful competition depends on freedom of sellers to enter into a business, if they can find a willing buyer, and on freedom of buyers to take their business where they will. Government licensing reduces competition by excluding many who would be able to find willing buyers, as it excluded Sharissa. Market discipline grows stronger as freedom of exchange is expanded.

Working together with customer experience are reputation and word of mouth, which give customers the benefit of experiences others have had with a particular hairdresser. Salons and salon franchises, such as the Hair Cuttery, work hard to establish and maintain a good reputation by giving good service.

Suppose a customer *is* injured while getting a haircut. In such cases—rare, we would hope and expect—the customer can sue for damages. Holding people accountable for the injury they do to another's property or person is a foundational legal institution on which a free market is based.

Salons themselves have a strong financial incentive to make sure injury never occurs, of course. Accordingly, they are likely to require some assurance of quality and competence *before* hiring. They might get that by observing the work of apprentices or by giving their own tests to applicants. More commonly, many salons might require some third-party certification of the hairdressers they hire, such as a diploma from a reputable beauty school. Such private-sector certification is fundamentally different from government licensing: it is voluntary rather than mandatory, so that if the certifier's requirements are excessive or inappropriate, the stylists and salons can turn elsewhere or do without. It is thus competitive rather than monopolized. Stylists and salons may choose from a variety of certifiers with different approaches and standards, rather than being forced to use the monopoly government licensing board. This competition tends to weed out requirements that don't actually benefit customers at acceptable cost. And because it is competitive, voluntary certification cannot be captured by a special-interest group.

Another kind of enterprise with a financial stake in safety and quality is insurance companies. The more competently and safely their clients work, the lower will be the payments insurance companies have to make to injured parties. Therefore, the insurers of hairdressers also have an incentive to require reasonable standards of hairdresser competence and training as a condition of providing insurance against lawsuit judgments.

In sum, in a totally free market for hairdressing, market forces would effectively regulate the quality and competence of hairdressers *without* being captured by existing hairdressers who use it to exclude competitors such as Sharissa and raise the prices their customers must pay.

Notice that all the market forces just mentioned are regulating hairdressing now, alongside the state governments' licensing requirements. Which of the two kinds of regulation do you suppose is more effective in ensuring the public health and safety, not to mention decent haircuts?

In a free market, these kinds of market forces would regulate the provision of virtually every good and service. Like other aspects of the free market, they wouldn't work perfectly because human beings are imperfect. But they would work well, much better than the top-down restrictions imposed by governments.

For readers who want to explore this subject further, I recommend Milton Friedman's discussion of licensing physicians in "Who Protects the Consumer?," Chapter 7 of *Free to Choose* (New York: Harcourt Brace Jovanovich, 1980), and Dan Klein and Alex Tabarrok's discussion of pharmaceuticals regulation on the FDAReview.org website (http://www.fdareview.org).

People Are Self-Interested in Public as in Private Life

People are self-interested—they pursue their personal well-being as they see it—in both private *and* public life. And in both settings, they make mistakes and sometimes behave badly.

This claim is at the heart of public choice economics. One of the founders of public choice, Nobel Laureate James Buchanan, has called it "politics without romance," because public choice rejects the tendency to contrast the imperfections of free-market processes with a romantic view of government intervention. Public choice does not presume that government interventions will accomplish their desired objectives. It compares the realities of the free market, with all its problems and imperfections, with the realities of government intervention, with all *its* problems and imperfections. Perfection is not available to imperfect human beings. In choosing between free markets and government intervention, we must ask ourselves not which is perfect, but which is preferable, or least bad, all things considered.

It was long implicitly assumed, in economic theories and civics textbooks, that "public servants" act in the public interest rather than in their own personal interest. No longer. Public choice economics has persuaded the economics profession that people who work in the public sector are as self-interested as people in the private sector. This assumption helps explain much of what goes on in government. To understand people's choices, in both public and private life, we should assume that they are self-interested, that they are trying to achieve their own personal goals at the lowest possible cost to themselves.

Given the inescapable self-interestedness of human beings, the key to a productive and cooperative social order is incentives that channel human beings' pursuit of their own self-interest into actions that benefit others at the same time. To this end, we need underlying institutions—basic rules of the game—that give everyone the incentive to cooperate with others and contribute to others' well-being as a way to advance their *own* interests. Private property and freedom of exchange are the core institutions that provide that incentive.

When society adheres closely to these institutions, the incentive to serve one's fellow man is much stronger than when government compulsion is in play. Where property must be respected and people are free to exchange with one another or not as they wish, people *must* serve others *in order* to achieve their own ends. Serving others is the only way we have to persuade others to give us what we want.

By contrast, the underlying institutions of government ownership and restriction of exchange give people perverse incentives to use government power for their own benefit at others' expense. Intervention establishes legal power to infringe on property rights and restrict peaceful, desired exchanges. That power is dangerous. Self-interested people in both the private and public sectors will be attracted to this government power; all of those in positions to gain from the intervention have strong, systematic, corrupting incentives to get what they want the easy way, regardless of the desires of their fellows.

The consequence of this insight for public policy is straightforward: No matter how good the intentions nor how important the aims of interference with private property or freedom of exchange, that interference is dangerous to the public well-being. It carries with it incentives for some people, usually in special-interest groups, to use the intervention for their own selfish purposes at the expense of the general public. It is preferable—it is safer for society—to avoid such interventions altogether. Any net good some particular intervention might do on occasion is more than offset by the net harm most interventions do most of the time. The safest course is to free our markets completely.

Conclusion

"More economic freedom means more human flourishing." So we said at the outset. In conclusion, let's review why this is so.

Human values are subjective; we value things differently. Hence, we can benefit one another by mutually exchanging what we value less for what we value more. In this sense, trade creates wealth.

The common idea that in a free economy some people (the rich, capitalists) benefit at the expense of others (the poor, workers, customers) is wrong. In a free economy, we all benefit one another—we create wealth for one another—in a vast network of mutually beneficial exchanges.

We also create wealth for one another by applying the ultimate resource—the human imagination coupled with the human spirit—to material resources, transforming those material resources into the goods and services that support and enrich our lives. Given time and freedom to use our creativity, the abundance people can create for one another has no limit.

At any point in time, however, goods are scarce, insufficient to satisfy all human wants for them. Every use of time and resources for one purpose means those resources cannot be used in the best alternative way; this is the opportunity cost of the action. Hence, we must economize. That is, we must seek to use additional—marginal—quantities of resources so as to create the most value from them.

How can we know how to economize so? What tells us how best to allocate marginal quantities of myriad different goods among myriad possible uses? Prices tell us. And profit and loss tell us.

Free-market prices emerge from the free interactions of sellers and buyers—supply and demand. Each seller and buyer has his or her own unique information about local conditions of needs for and supplies of any particular good, and this knowledge is reflected in the price he or she is willing to bid or ask for it. As sellers compete by offering to sell for less and buyers compete by offering to pay more, a going market price is generated that tells an important story. In a way, it summarizes the local knowledge of all the different buyers and sellers. It tells us the value of (one more unit of) that good to the last person willing to buy and the cost of (one more unit of) that good to the last person willing to sell. Thus, that price reflects the current availability of and need for that good. With that precious piece of information—that price—we can economize. We can use goods only where the value of doing so exceeds the cost.

Interference with market prices is always a bad idea, because it blocks the flow of information about values and costs. Price controls prevent prices from telling their stories about the current availability of and need for the goods or services whose prices are controlled.

Using free-market prices, businesspeople can calculate profit and loss, their guide for discovering how best to create value for others. Profit means that the value to customers of a project's output exceeds the opportunity cost of the resources it uses up. Profit, in free and informed exchange, comes from creating new value for others, whereas loss comes from destroying value. In a world where the future is uncertain—where even the experts can't know for sure what to do today to make the world a better place tomorrow—and where there are limited resources to invest, profit and loss select among entrepreneurial innovations and guide the process of creative destruction on which rising standards of living depend.

Private ownership and freedom of exchange, the foundational institutions of free societies, make possible the prices and profits and losses that tell us how best to serve others. They also give us the incentive to do so. Where governments respect and protect everyone's justly acquired property and all are free to exchange with others, or not, as they see fit, the only way for one person to get what he or she wants from others is to give others what they want in exchange. Thus, free markets constantly push people to promote the well-being of others. The trouble with even well-intended government intervention—which means the use of force to mandate unwanted exchanges or to forbid desired exchanges—is that it tempts people to use that government power to get what they want against the well-being of others. People don't handle that power well.

Economics teaches us that free markets foster human cooperation and human flourishing. With the knowledge that free-market prices give us, the guidance that free-market profit and loss give us, and the incentives that private ownership and freedom of exchange give us, we are all led by Adam Smith's invisible hand to specialize, produce abundantly, and trade with one another to mutual advantage in a marvelous extended order of human cooperation.

Endnotes

1. From *Basic Economics*, quoted at *Cafe Hayek* (blog), http://cafehayek.com/2006/05/sowell_on_scarc.html.

2. This example is taken from James D. Gwartney et al., *Microeconomics, Private and Public Choice*, 15th ed. (Stamford, CT: Cengage Learning, 2015), pp. 302–304.

3. Ilyce R. Glink, "Top 10 Priciest U.S. Cities to Rent an Apartment," *CBS MoneyWatch*, July 15, 2013, http://www.cbsnews.com/media/top-10-priciest-us-cities-to-rent-an-apartment/.

4. George A. Selgin, *The Theory of Free Banking: Money Supply under Competitive Note Issue* (Lanham, MD.: Rowman & Littlefield, 1988), p. 93.

5. Tyler Cowen and Alex Tabarrok, *Modern Principles of Microeconomics*, 2nd ed. (New York: Worth Publishers, 2013), p. 113.

6. Personal correspondence.

7. F. A. Hayek. "The Use of Knowledge in Society," *American Economic Review* 35 no. 4 (September 1945): 519–30.

8. An accessible, short explication of the source of profit is Fred I. Kent's "Letter to his Grandson," April 1942, available at http://www.freemarketfoundation.com/article-view/letter-to-his-grandson.

The work to which I am most indebted for the presentation in this chapter is Ludwig von Mises's "Profit and Loss," in *Planning for Freedom* (South Holland, IL: Libertarian Press, 1952), available at https://mises.org/library/profit-and-loss-0.

9. The size of this "bargain" is called "consumer surplus" in the textbooks.

10. The original company was called Iridium LLC. Its assets were bought out of bankruptcy in December 2000 by a new company called Iridium Satellite LLC, which was immediately awarded a two-year, $72 million contract with the Department of Defense for unlimited use of the low-Earth-orbit network. Note that that $72 million is approximately 1.15 percent of the low-end estimate of $5 billion spent building the system. The Department of Defense is still the company's main customer. Since a merger in 2009, the company has been called Iridium Communications, Inc. More information is available at Iridum's website and at http://archive.defense.gov/releases/release.aspx?releaseid=2769.

11. Joseph Schumpeter, *Capitalism, Socialism, and Democracy* (New York: Harper & Brothers Publishers, 1950), p. 83.

12. Franz Oppenheimer, *The State*, first published in German in 1908. *The State: Its History and Development Viewed Sociologically,* trans. John M. Gitterman (New York: B. W. Huebsch, 1922), is available from the Online Library of Liberty at http://oll.libertyfund.org/title/1662.

13. John Baden, *Destroying the Environment: Government Mismanagement of Our Natural Resources*, National Center for Policy Analysis, Policy Report No. 124 (October, 1986) pp. 12–13.

14. The Forest Service's website about the Tongass used to contain a FAQ page which was the source of much of the data in this section. It was located on the web at http://www.fs.fed.us/r10/tongass/forest_facts/faqs/forestmgmt.shtml. That page has been taken down. Any reader wishing to see it may email the author for a copy.

15. Baden, p. 9.

16. Baden, p. 34.

Recommended Readings

Henry Hazlitt, *Economics in One Lesson.* Rightly billed as "the shortest and surest way to understand basic economics," this book has been the most valuable book in my economics education. In short, lucid chapters, it teaches how to think about economic policies and problems such as taxes, tariffs, subsidies, rent controls, minimum wage laws, unions, profits, and inflation. It's superb.

Thomas Sowell, *Basic Economics.* This book, appropriately subtitled "A Common Sense Guide to the Economy," is a rich and rewarding exploration of the fundamental facts and principles of economics. Its engaging writing and broad range of illustrative examples make learning economics relaxed and enjoyable.

Howard Baetjer Jr., *Free Our Markets*. The freer the markets people live in, the better they flourish. This book explains why that is so, in terms of foundational economic principles. Free of graphs and economic jargon, it uses thought experiments and examples to give the reader an intuitive understanding of spontaneous economic order.

About the Author

Howard Baetjer Jr. is a Lecturer in the Department of Economics at Towson University, where he teaches microeconomics, money and banking, comparative economic systems, and the history of economic thought. He is the author of *Free Our Markets: A Citizens' Guide to Essential Economics* (Jane Philip Publications, 2013) and *Software as Capital: An Economic Perspective on Software Engineering* (IEEE Computer Society, 1998). He holds a BA in psychology from Princeton (1974), an MLitt in English literature from the University of Edinburgh (1980), and MA in political science from Boston College (1984), and a PhD in economics from George Mason University (1993).

Index

Note: Page numbers with letter f, n, or t indicate figures, notes, or tables, respectively.

Libertarianism.org

Liberty. It's a simple idea and the linchpin of a complex system of values and practices: justice, prosperity, responsibility, toleration, cooperation, and peace. Many people believe that liberty is the core political value of modern civilization itself, the one that gives substance and form to all the other values of social life. They're called libertarians.

Libertarianism.org is the Cato Institute's treasury of resources about the theory and history of liberty. The book you're holding is a small part of what Libertarianism.org has to offer. In addition to hosting classic texts by historical libertarian figures and original articles from modern-day thinkers, Libertarianism.org publishes podcasts, videos, online introductory courses, and books on a variety of topics within the libertarian tradition.

Cato Institute

Founded in 1977, the Cato Institute is a public policy research foundation dedicated to broadening the parameters of policy debate to allow consideration of more options that are consistent with the principles of limited government, individual liberty, and peace. To that end, the Institute strives to achieve greater involvement of the intelligent, concerned lay public in questions of policy and the proper role of government.

The Institute is named for *Cato's Letters*, libertarian pamphlets that were widely read in the American Colonies in the early 18th century and played a major role in laying the philosophical foundation for the American Revolution.

Despite the achievement of the nation's Founders, today virtually no aspect of life is free from government encroachment. A pervasive intolerance for individual rights is shown by government's arbitrary intrusions into private economic transactions and its disregard for civil liberties. And while freedom around the globe has notably increased in the past several decades, many countries have moved in the opposite direction, and most governments still do not respect or safeguard the wide range of civil and economic liberties.

To address those issues, the Cato Institute undertakes an extensive publications program on the complete spectrum of policy issues. Books, monographs, and shorter studies are commissioned to examine the federal budget, Social Security, regulation, military spending, international trade, and myriad other issues. Major policy conferences are held throughout the year, from which papers are published thrice yearly in the *Cato Journal*. The Institute also publishes the quarterly magazine *Regulation*.

In order to maintain its independence, the Cato Institute accepts no government funding. Contributions are received from foundations, corporations, and individuals, and other revenue is generated from the sale of publications. The Institute is a nonprofit, tax-exempt, educational foundation under Section 501(c)3 of the Internal Revenue Code.

CATO INSTITUTE
1000 Massachusetts Ave., N.W.
Washington, D.C. 20001
www.cato.org

CPSIA information can be obtained
at www.ICGtesting.com
Printed in the USA
BVHW032045110821
614096BV00012BA/601